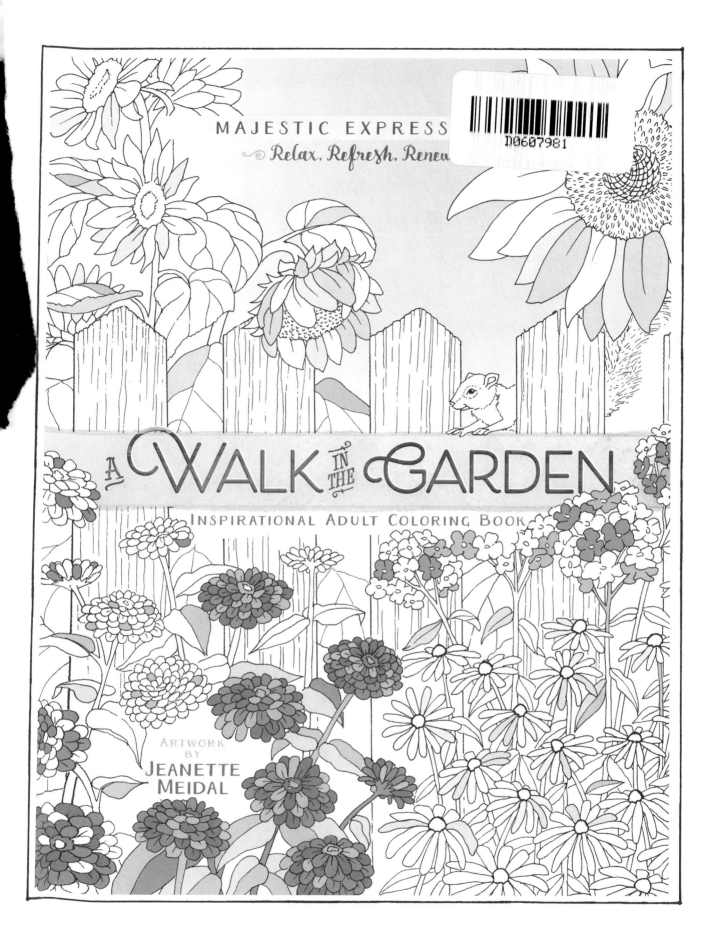

MAJESTIC EXPRESS
Relax, Refresh, Renew

A WALK IN THE GARDEN

INSPIRATIONAL ADULT COLORING BOOK

ARTWORK
BY
JEANETTE
MEIDAL

BroadStreet
PUBLISHING

BroadStreet Publishing Group LLC
Racine, Wisconsin, USA
Broadstreetpublishing.com

MAJESTIC EXPRESSIONS

A WALK IN THE GARDEN

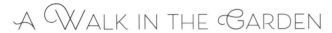

© 2016 by BroadStreet Publishing

ISBN 978-1-4245-5223-8

Artwork by Jeanette Meidal.

Cover design by Chris Garborg | garborgdesign.com
Compiled and edited by Michelle Winger | literallyprecise.com

Printed in the United States of America.

16 17 18 19 20 21 22   7 6 5 4 3 2 1

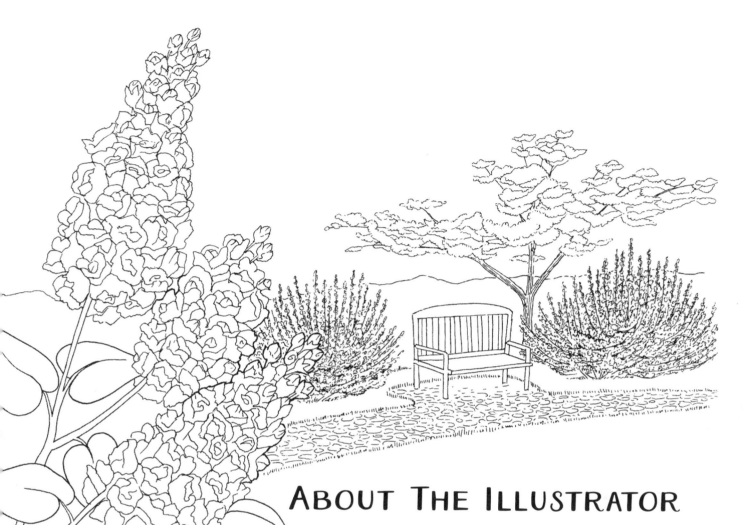

ABOUT THE ILLUSTRATOR

JEANETTE MEIDAL delights in sharing the artistic gifts

God has given her with others, to bless them and to bring glory to

him. She has been an art educator for students of all ages and loves

making original greeting cards. She is inspired by the beauty of

God's creation and enjoys observing nature, gardening, and playing

the violin. Jeanette and her husband live in Minnesota. They have

three grown sons and three wonderful granddaughters.

Dear Julia

Enjoy the comfort of coloring

Love Betty K

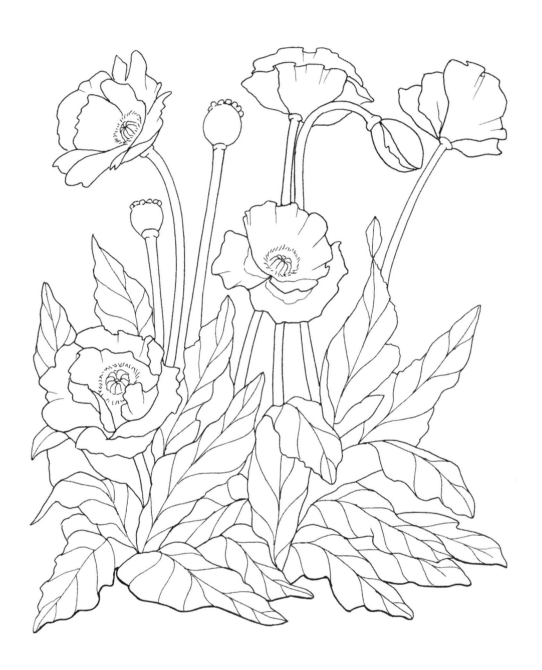

INTRODUCTION

WHY ADULT COLORING BOOKS?

There is plenty of research that shows coloring to be an effective stress reducer. Maybe you picked up this book because you've heard the hype and you're curious. Perhaps you've been looking for a way to relax. Or, if you're like many others we've encountered, you've been looking for a good excuse to color since you "grew up" and coloring books were no longer an acceptable hobby. Over the years, you may have found yourself eager to babysit kids who were fond of coloring, or maybe you have children or grandchildren of your own that need your help filling in the pages of their coloring books.

Finally you hold in your hand your very own adult coloring book. And you have every reason you need to sit down and color. You have entered a stress-free zone. There's no wrong way to color. If you want the grass to be blue and the sky to be green, go right ahead. If you only want to color a portion of a picture, do it. Crayons? Coloring pencils? Markers? It's your choice. This is your book, and this is your time.

Let's take it a step further. While coloring may be a great distraction from all you have going on, the best way to find lasting peace is to spend time with your Creator. As you fill these intricately designed illustrations with the beauty of color, dwell on richness of his Word, the faithfulness of his character, and the depth of his love for you.

"I HAVE TOLD YOU THESE THINGS, SO THAT IN ME YOU MAY HAVE PEACE.
IN THIS WORLD YOU WILL HAVE TROUBLE.
BUT TAKE HEART! I HAVE OVERCOME THE WORLD."
JOHN 16:33 NIV

Happy coloring!

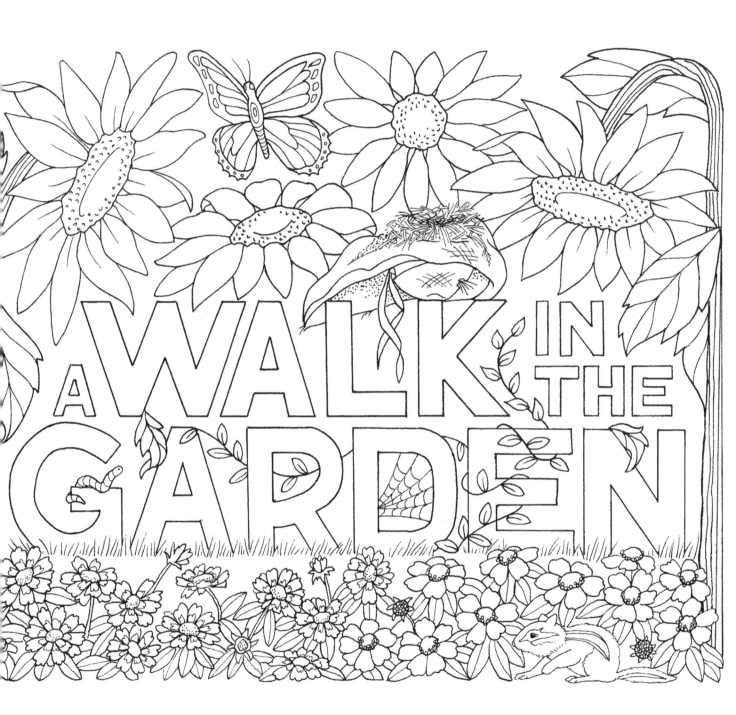

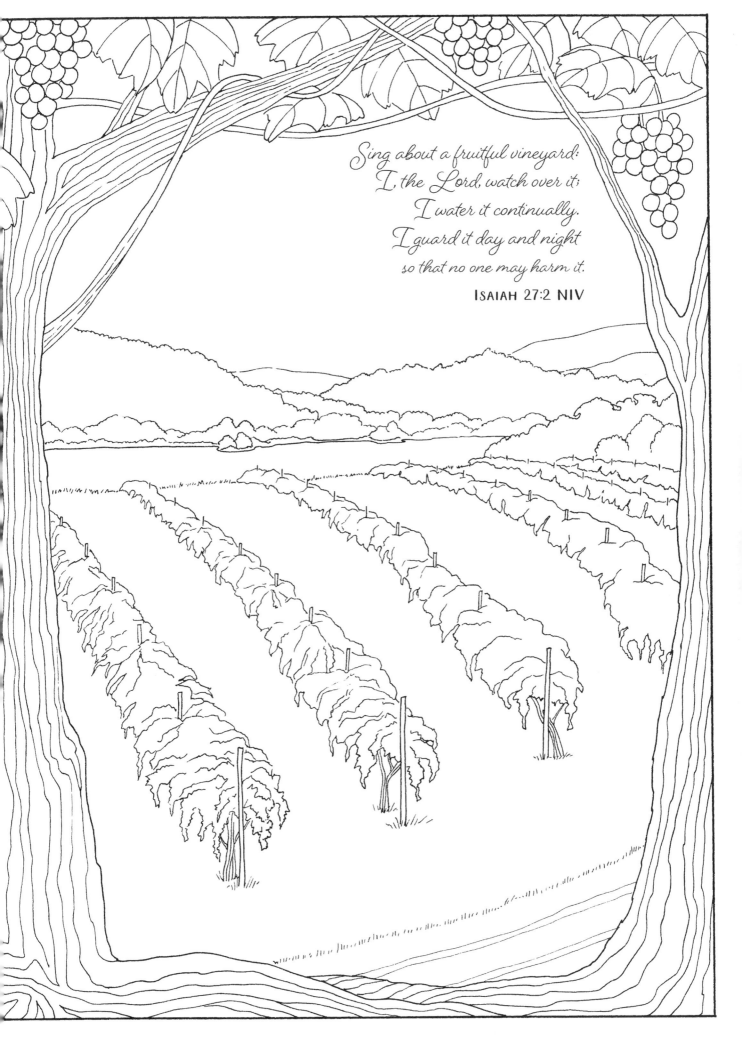

Sing about a fruitful vineyard:
I, the Lord, watch over it;
I water it continually.
I guard it day and night
so that no one may harm it.

ISAIAH 27:2 NIV

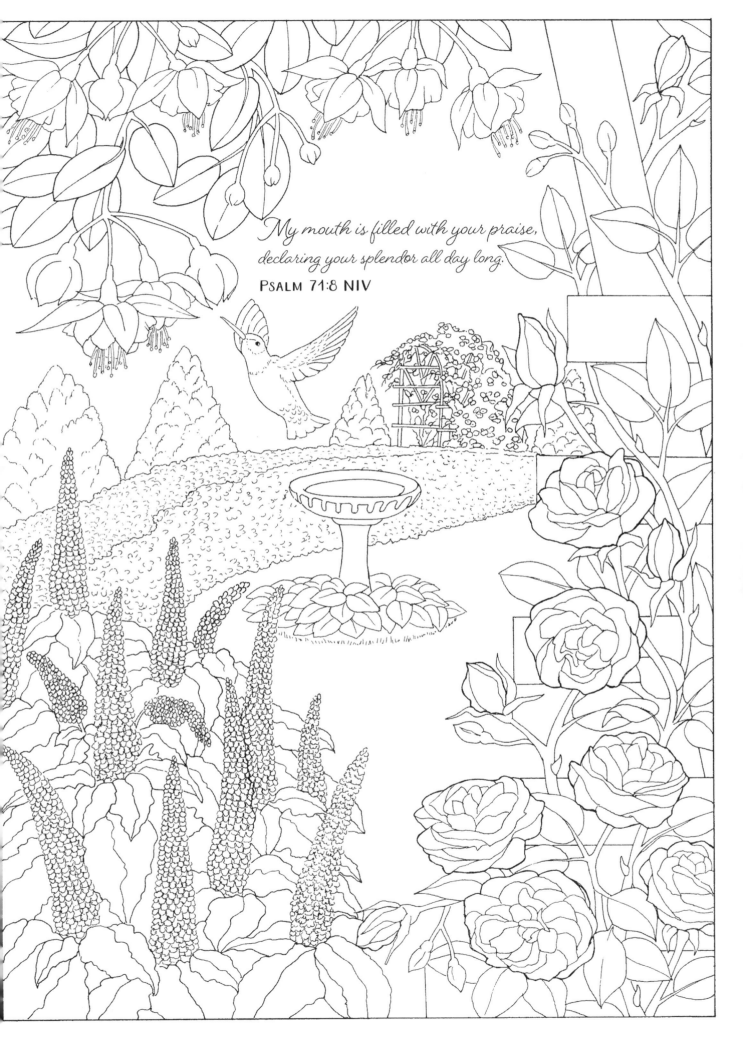

My mouth is filled with your praise,
declaring your splendor all day long.

PSALM 71:8 NIV

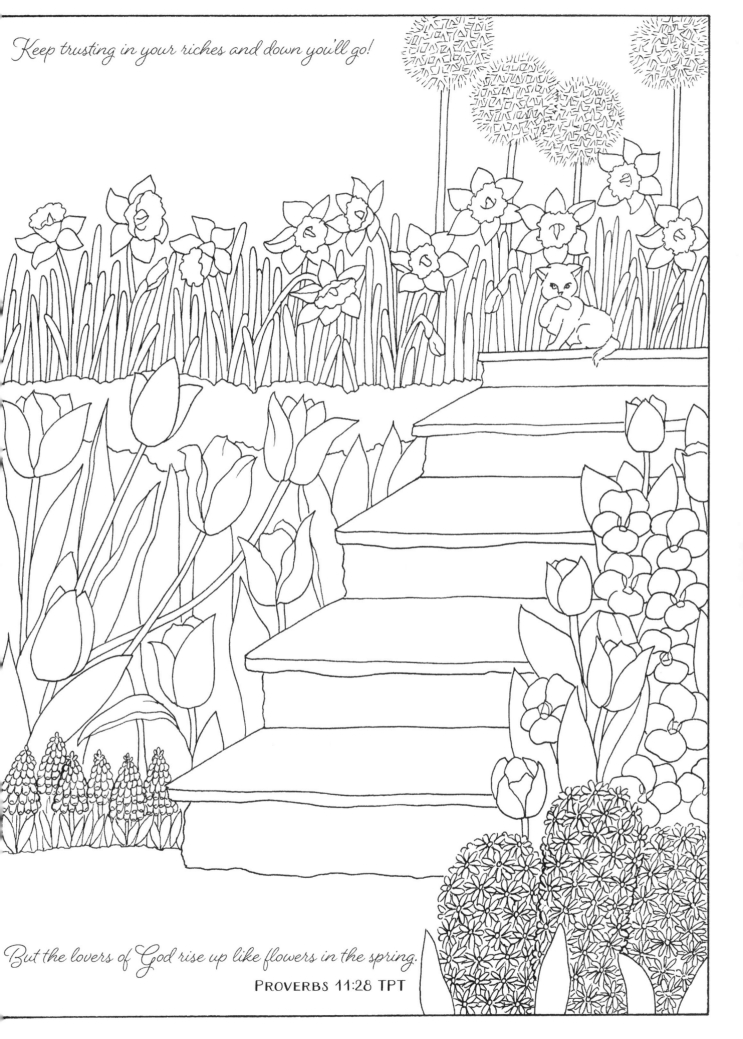

Keep trusting in your riches and down you'll go!

But the lovers of God rise up like flowers in the spring.
PROVERBS 11:28 TPT

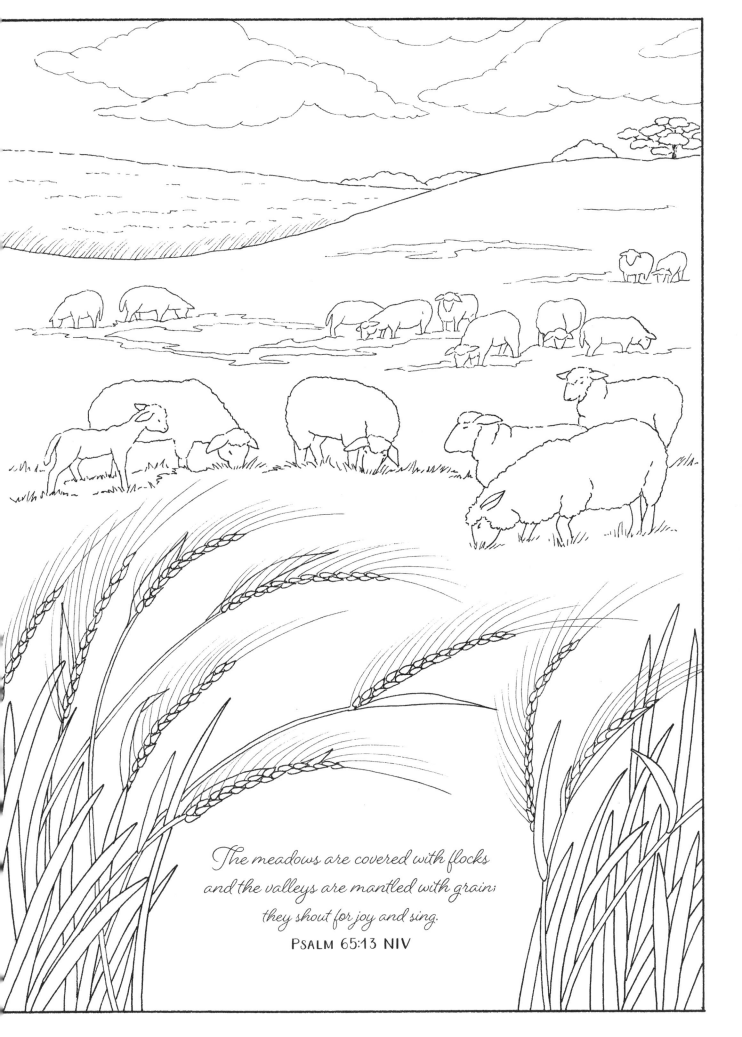

The meadows are covered with flocks
and the valleys are mantled with grain;
they shout for joy and sing.
PSALM 65:13 NIV

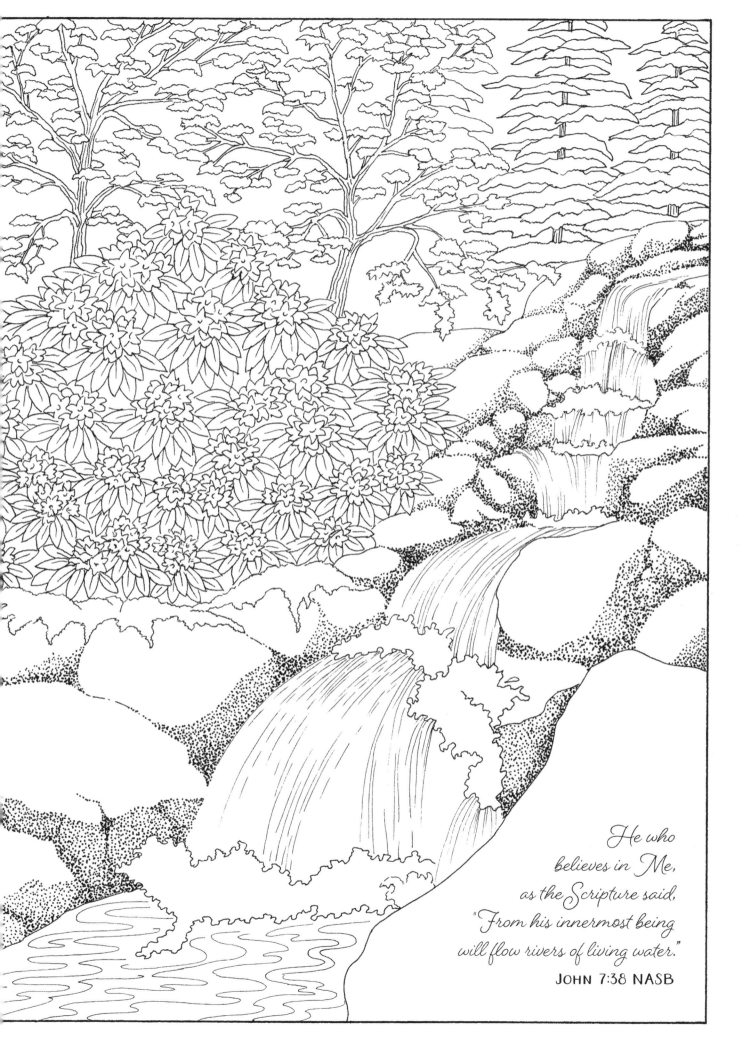

*He who
believes in Me,
as the Scripture said,
"From his innermost being
will flow rivers of living water."*

JOHN 7:38 NASB

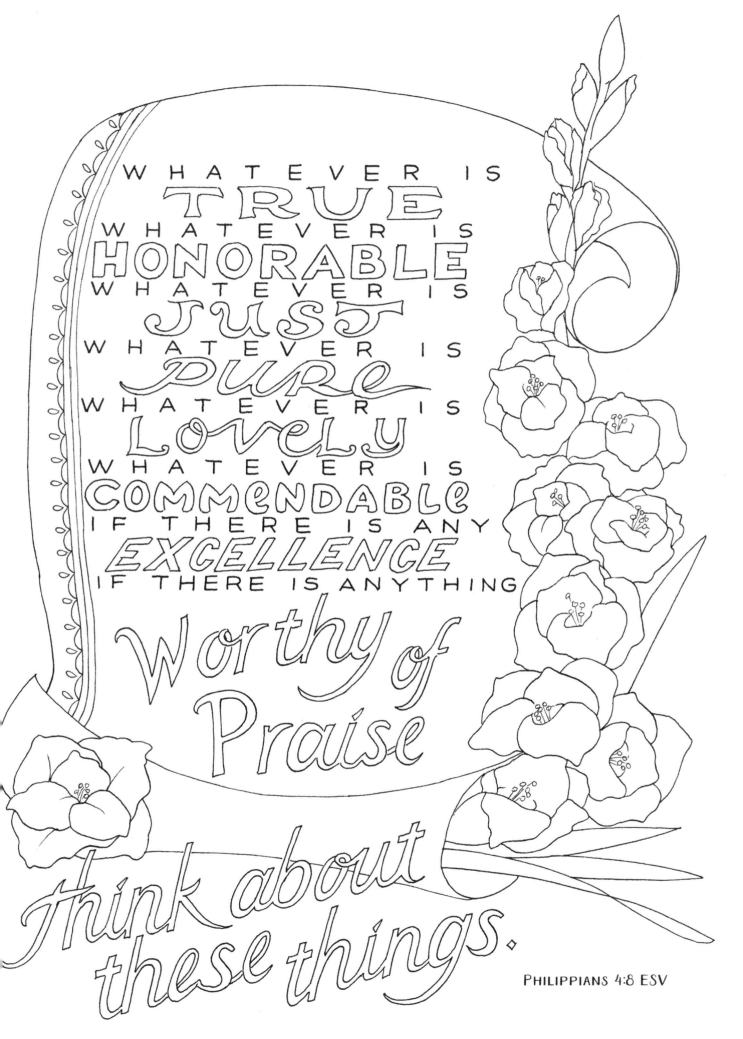

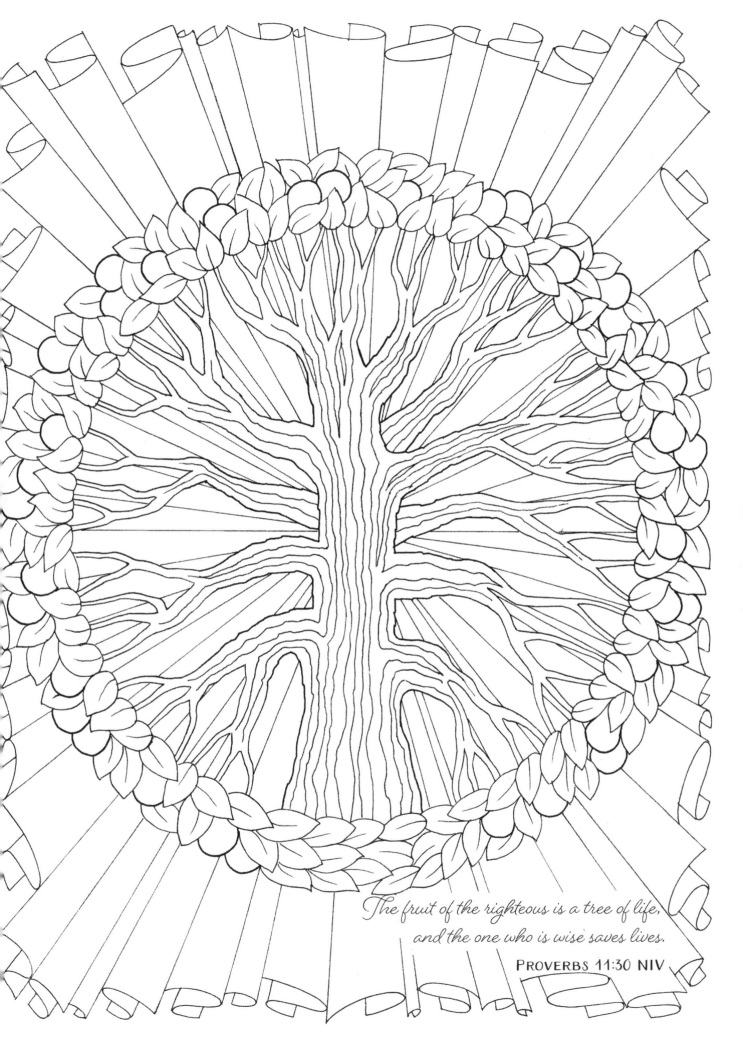

*The fruit of the righteous is a tree of life,
and the one who is wise saves lives.*

PROVERBS 11:30 NIV

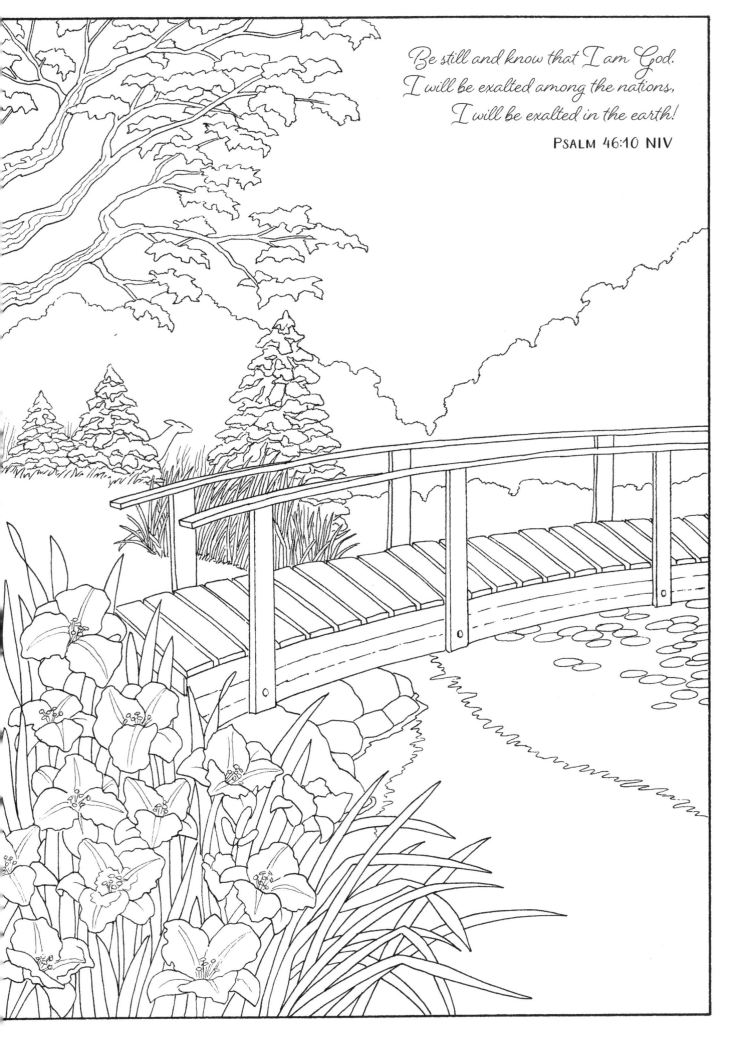

Be still and know that I am God.
I will be exalted among the nations,
I will be exalted in the earth!

PSALM 46:10 NIV

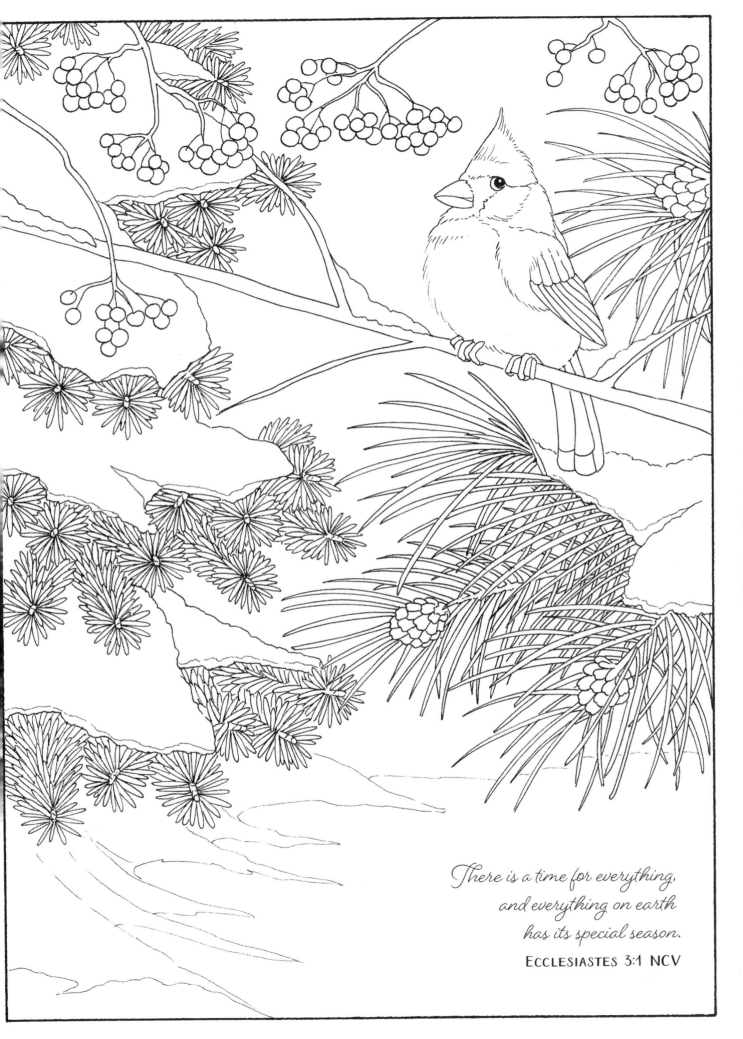

*There is a time for everything,
and everything on earth
has its special season.*
ECCLESIASTES 3:1 NCV

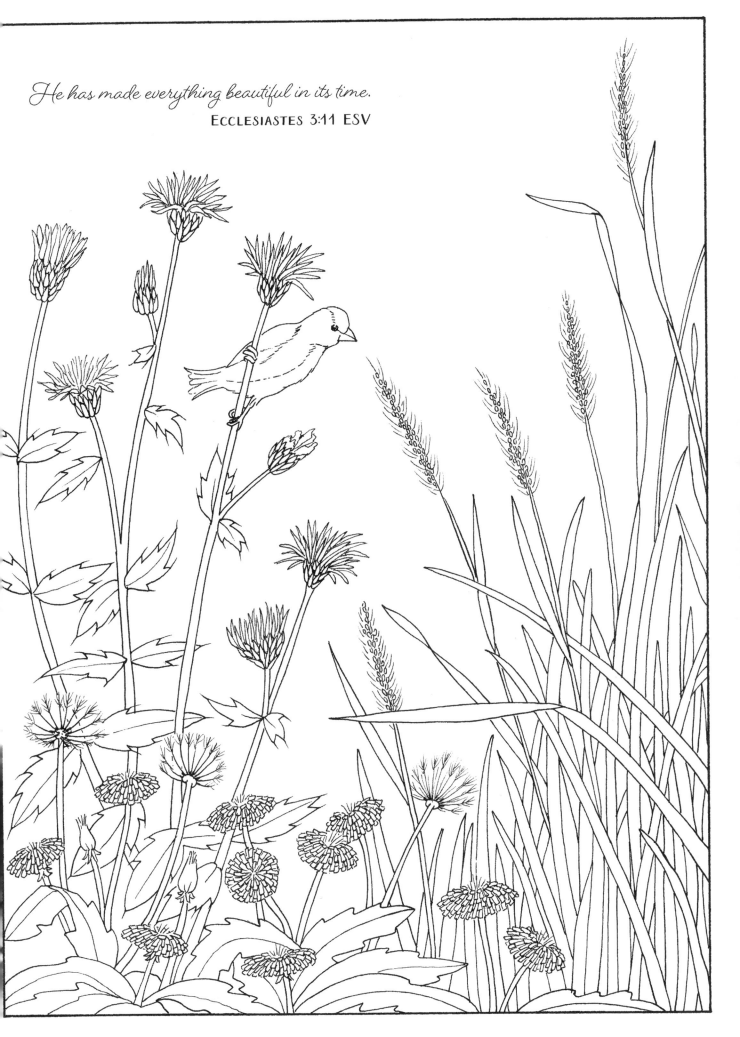

He has made everything beautiful in its time.
ECCLESIASTES 3:11 ESV

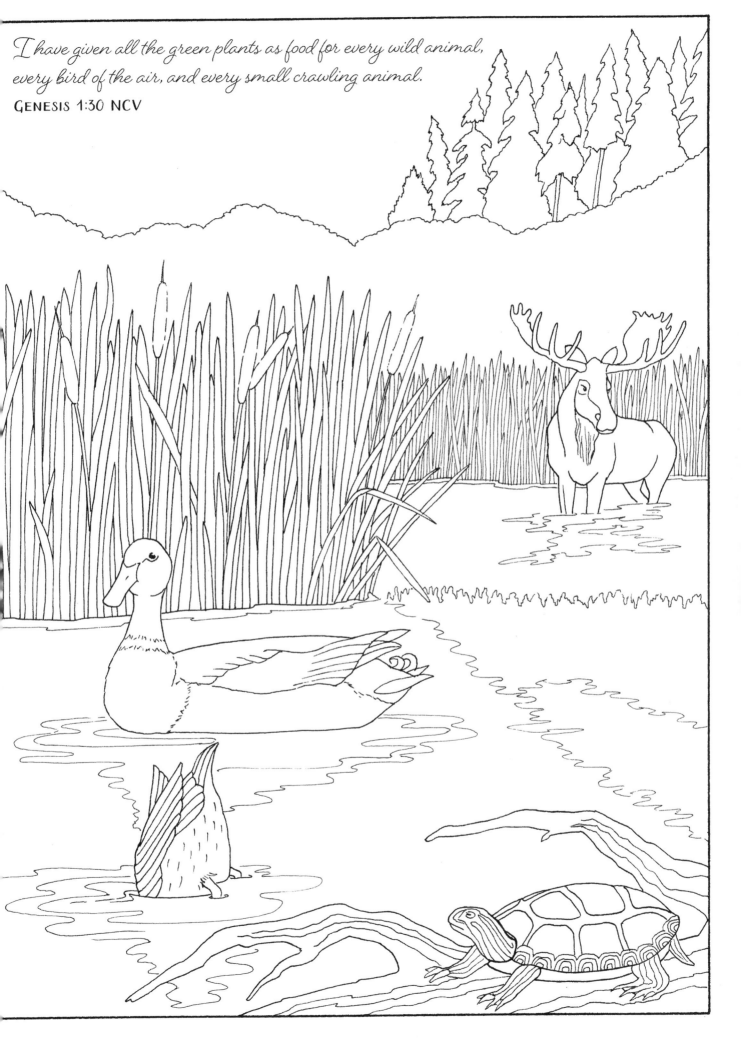

I have given all the green plants as food for every wild animal, every bird of the air, and every small crawling animal.
GENESIS 1:30 NCV

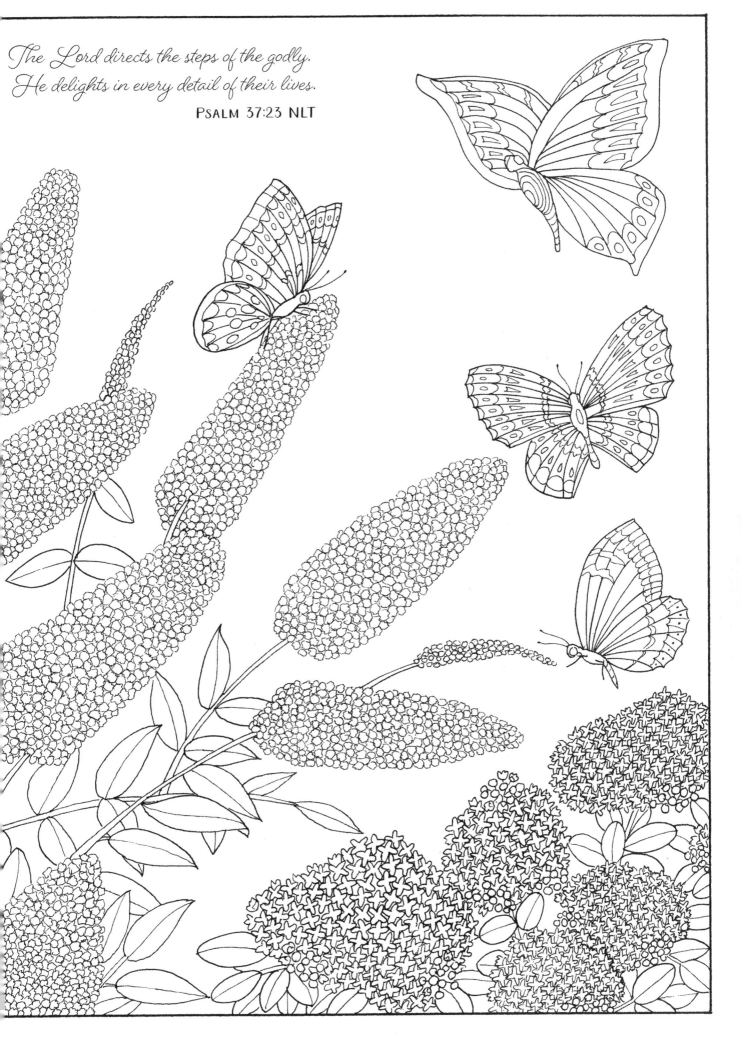

The Lord directs the steps of the godly.
He delights in every detail of their lives.

PSALM 37:23 NLT

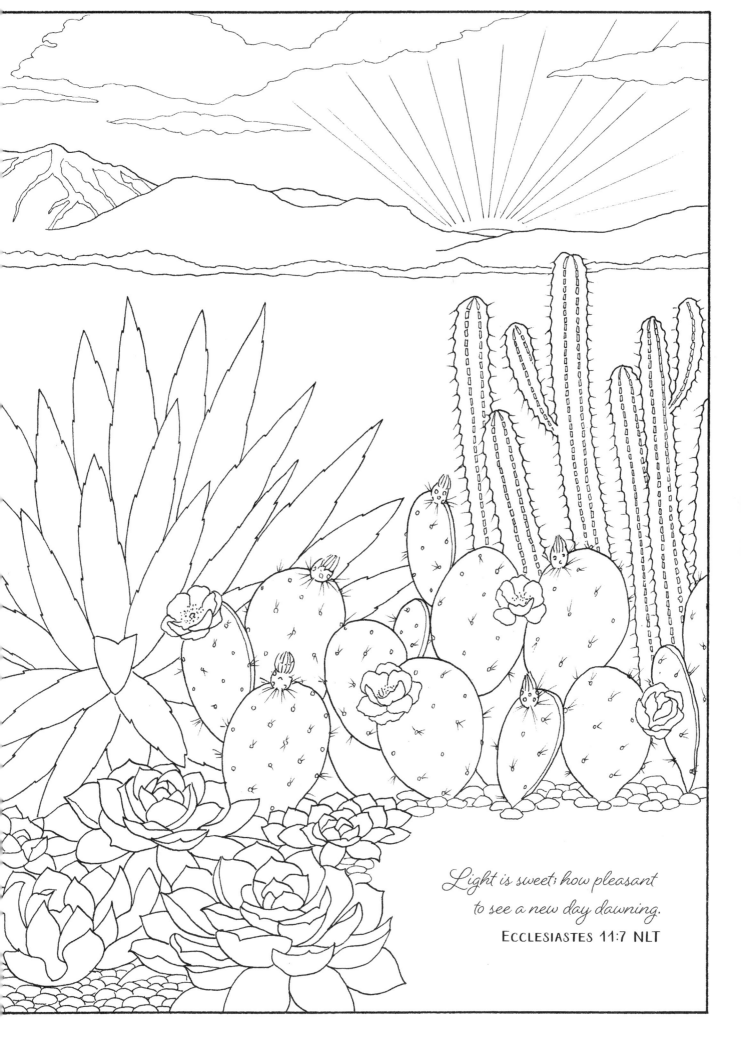

*Light is sweet; how pleasant
to see a new day dawning.*
ECCLESIASTES 11:7 NLT

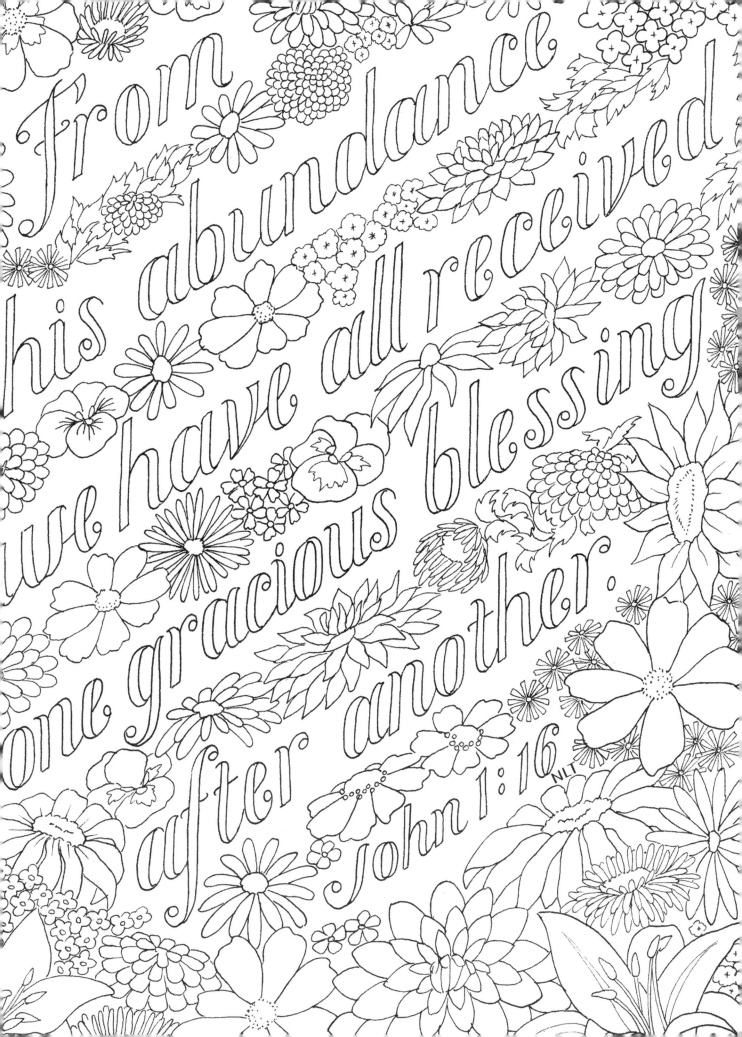

From his abundance we have all received one gracious blessing after another. John 1:16 NLT

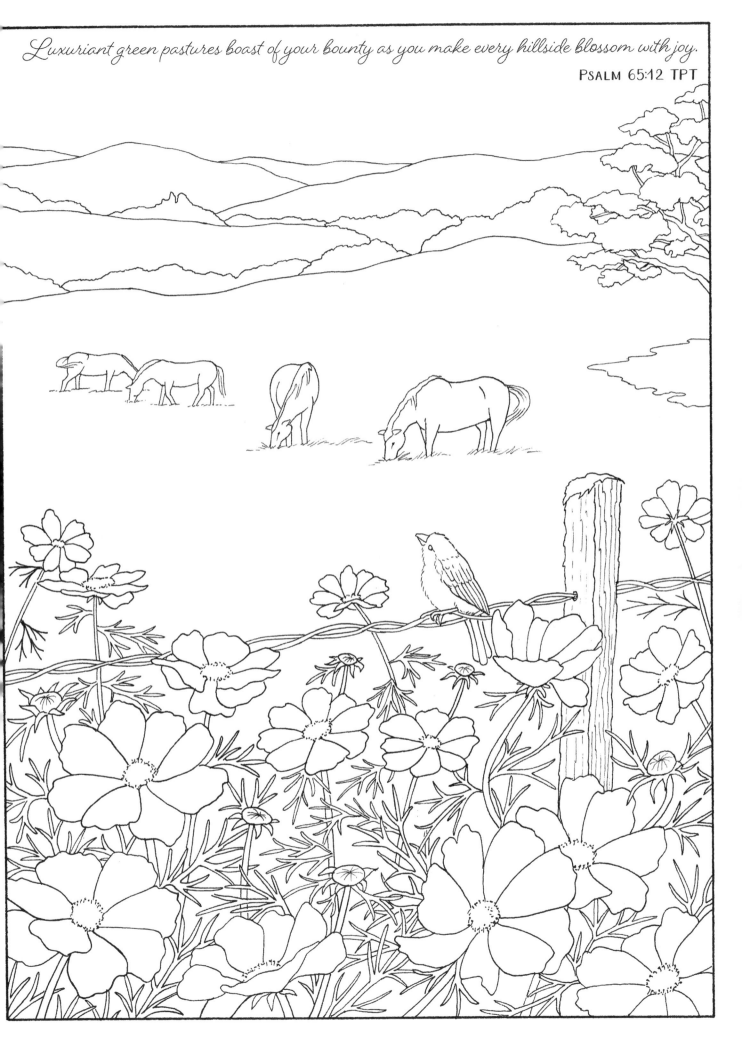

Luxuriant green pastures boast of your bounty as you make every hillside blossom with joy.

PSALM 65:12 TPT

Everything I am will praise and bless the Lord!
O Lord, my God, your greatness takes my breath away,
overwhelming me by your majesty, beauty, and splendor!

PSALM 104:1 TPT

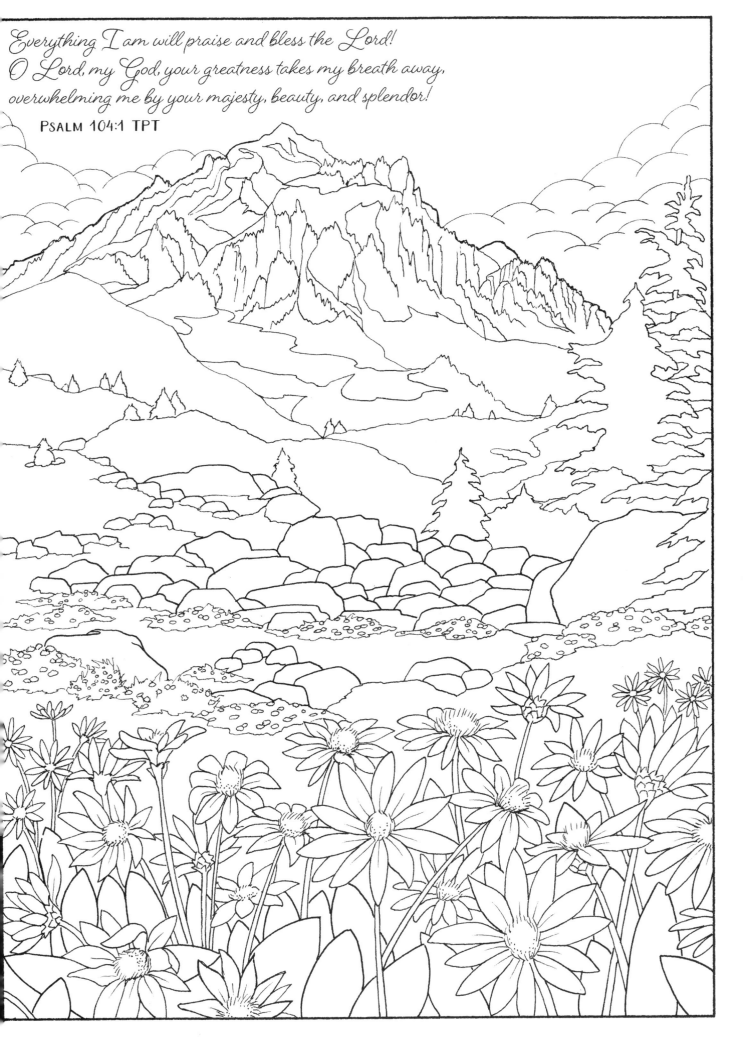

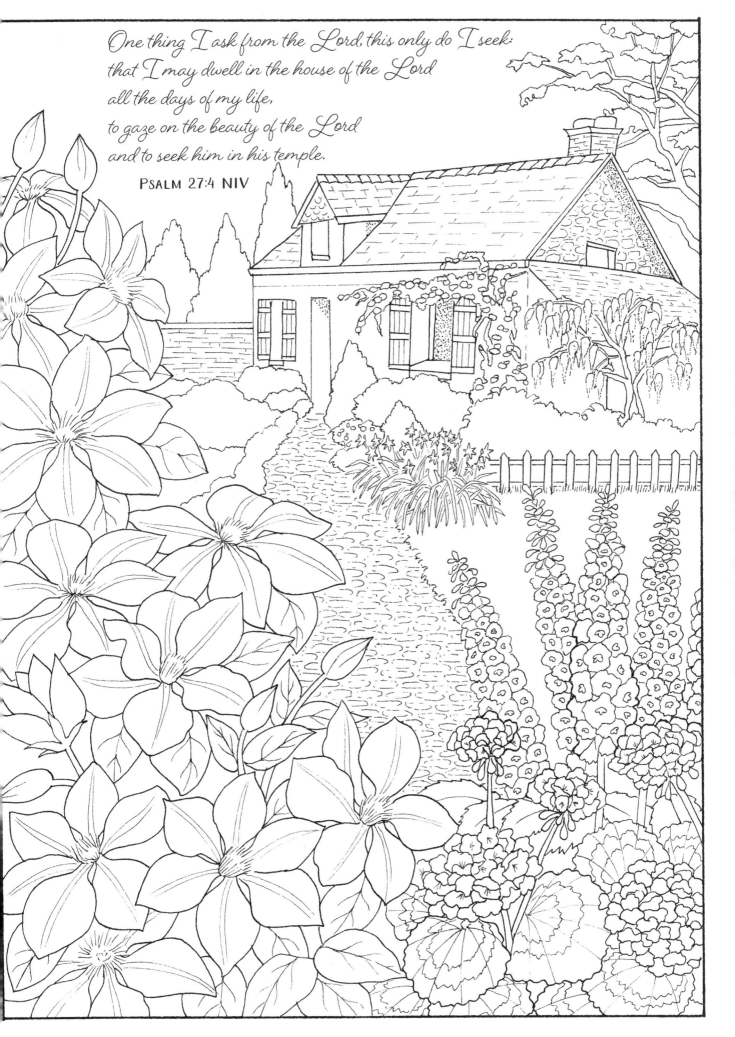

One thing I ask from the Lord, this only do I seek:
that I may dwell in the house of the Lord
all the days of my life,
to gaze on the beauty of the Lord
and to seek him in his temple.

PSALM 27:4 NIV

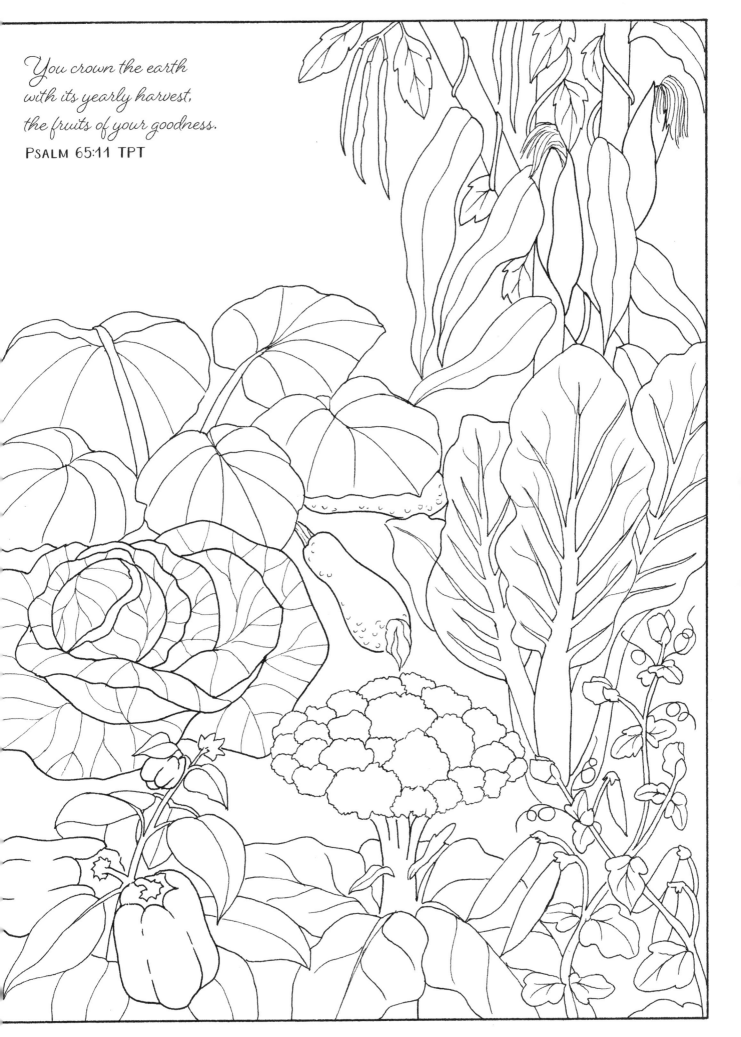

You crown the earth
with its yearly harvest,
the fruits of your goodness.
PSALM 65:11 TPT

*Every field is watered with the abundance of rain—
showers soaking the earth and softening its clods,
causing seeds to sprout throughout the land.*

PSALM 65:10 TPT

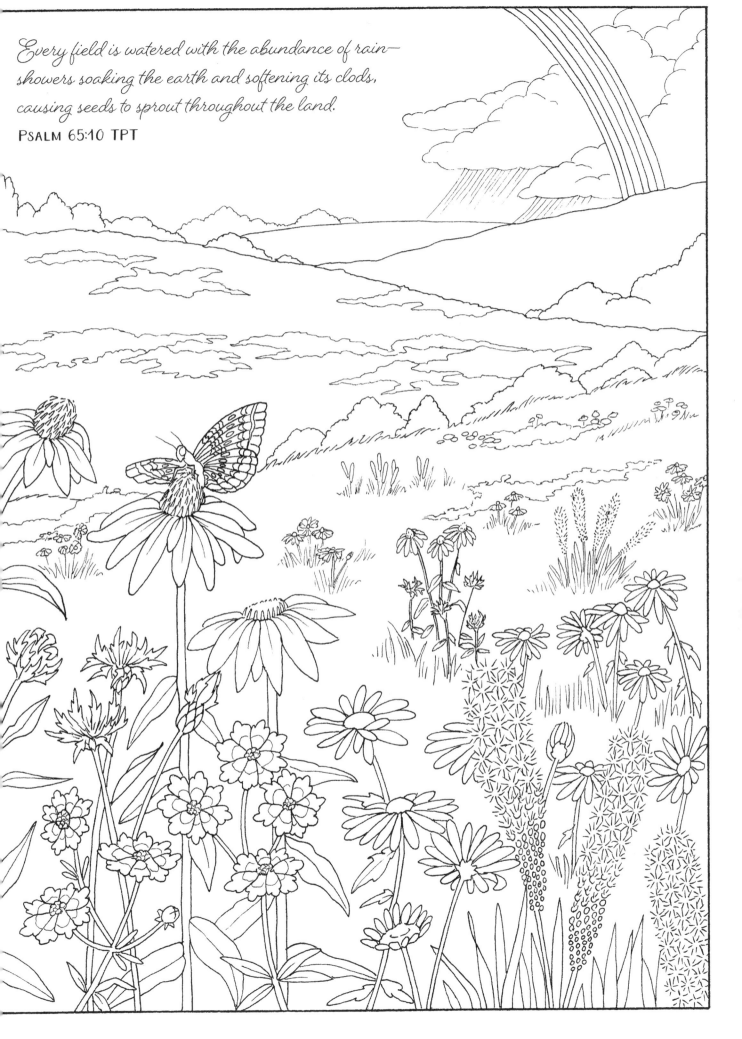

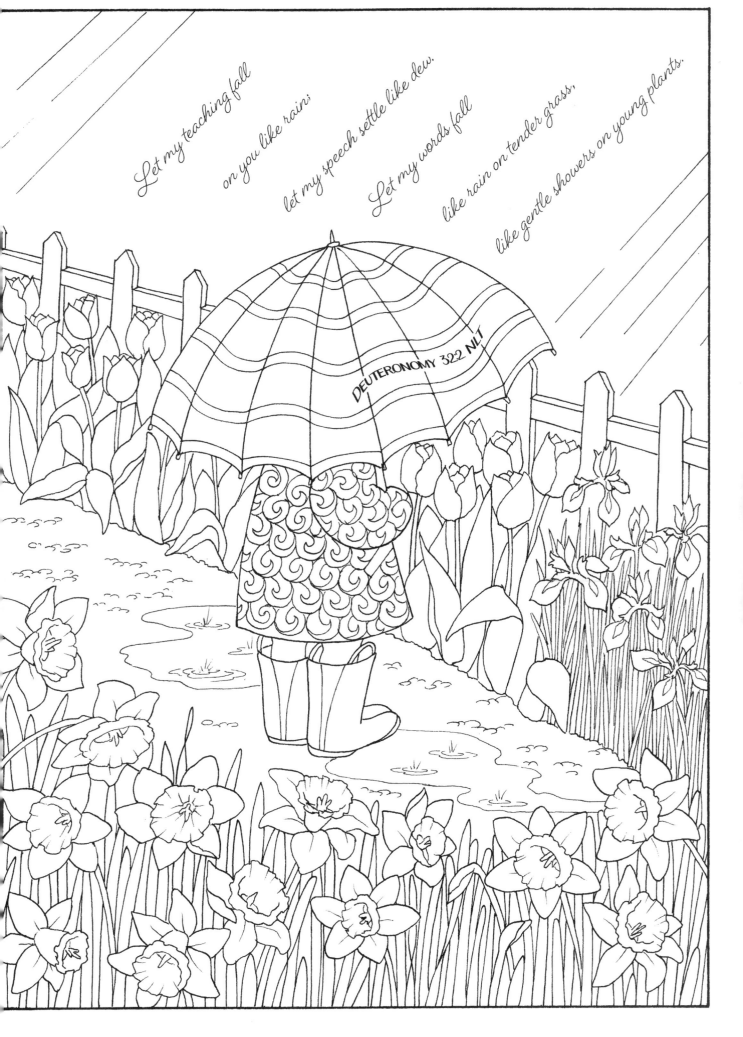

Let my teaching fall on you like rain; let my speech settle like dew. Let my words fall like rain on tender grass, like gentle showers on young plants.

DEUTERONOMY 32:2 NLT

Isaiah 40:8 ESV

The grass withers

the flowers fade

BUT THE WORD OF OUR GOD STANDS FOREVER

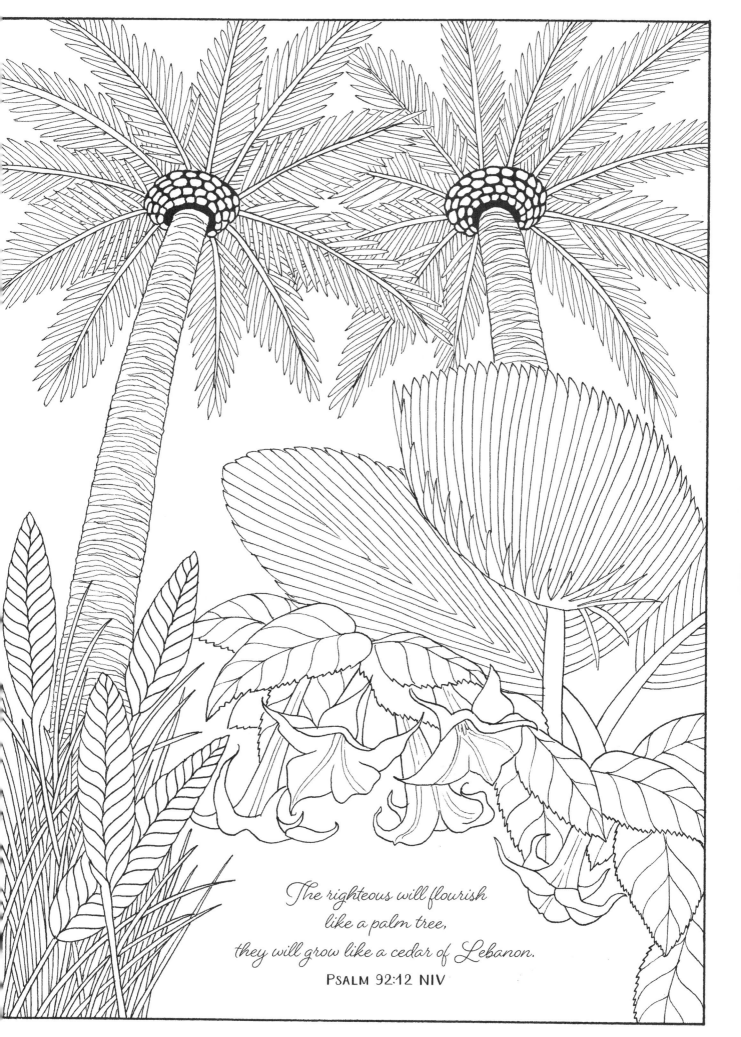

*The righteous will flourish
like a palm tree,
they will grow like a cedar of Lebanon.*

PSALM 92:12 NIV

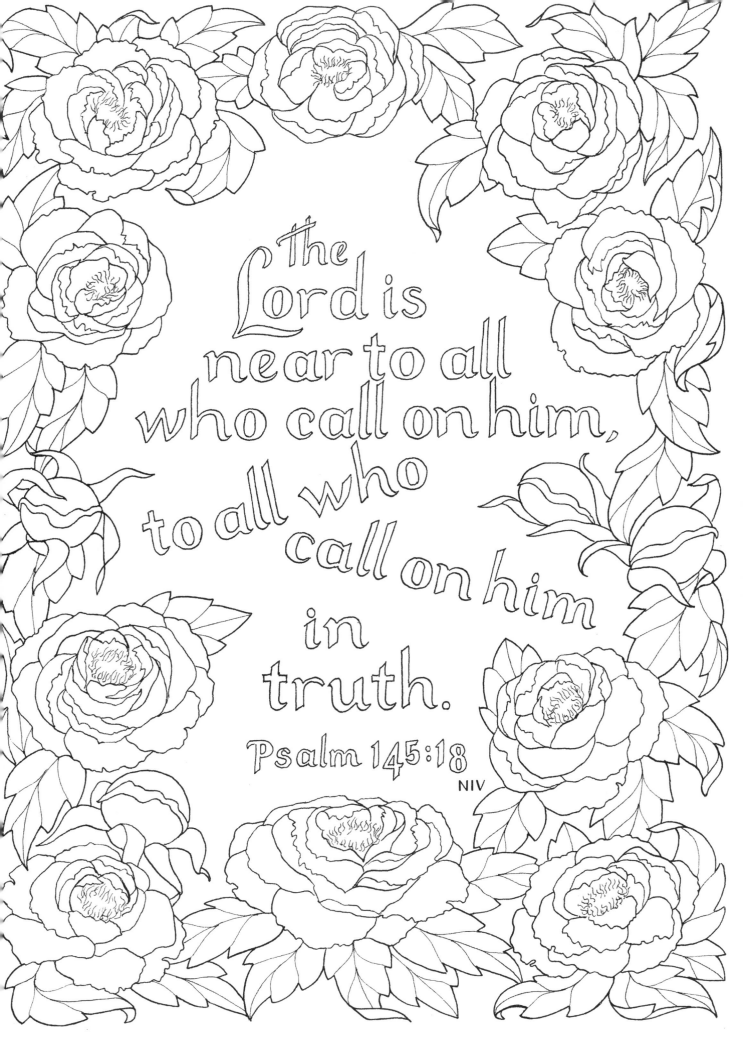

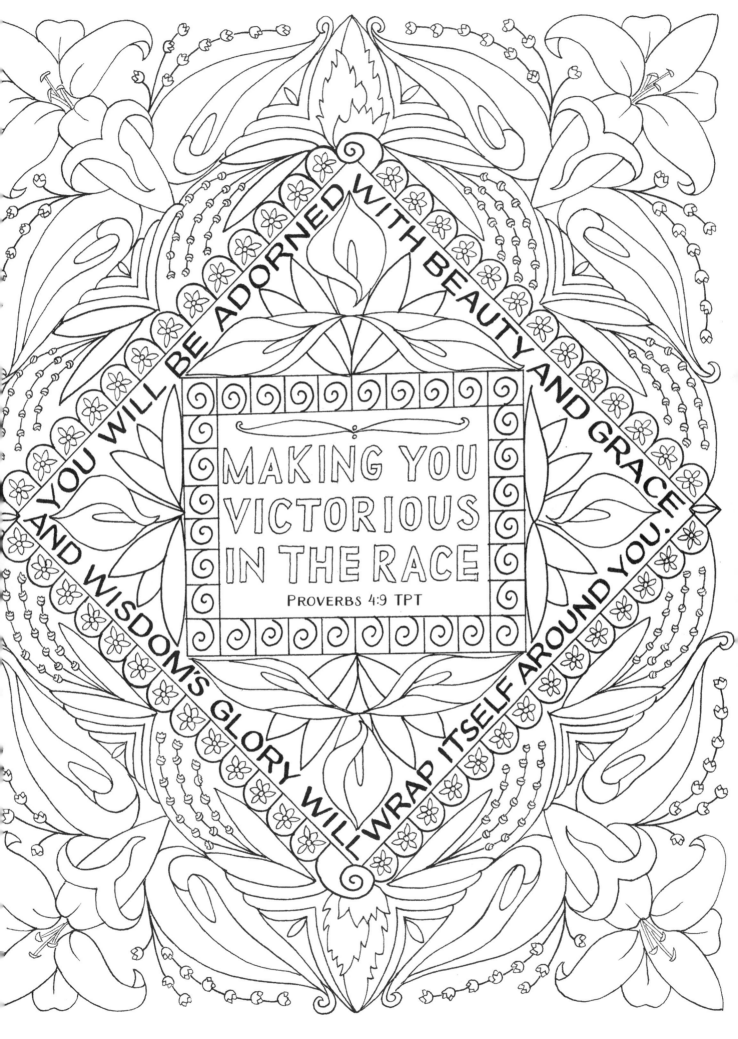

YOU WILL BE ADORNED WITH BEAUTY AND GRACE. AND WISDOM'S GLORY WILL WRAP ITSELF AROUND YOU.

MAKING YOU VICTORIOUS IN THE RACE

PROVERBS 4:9 TPT

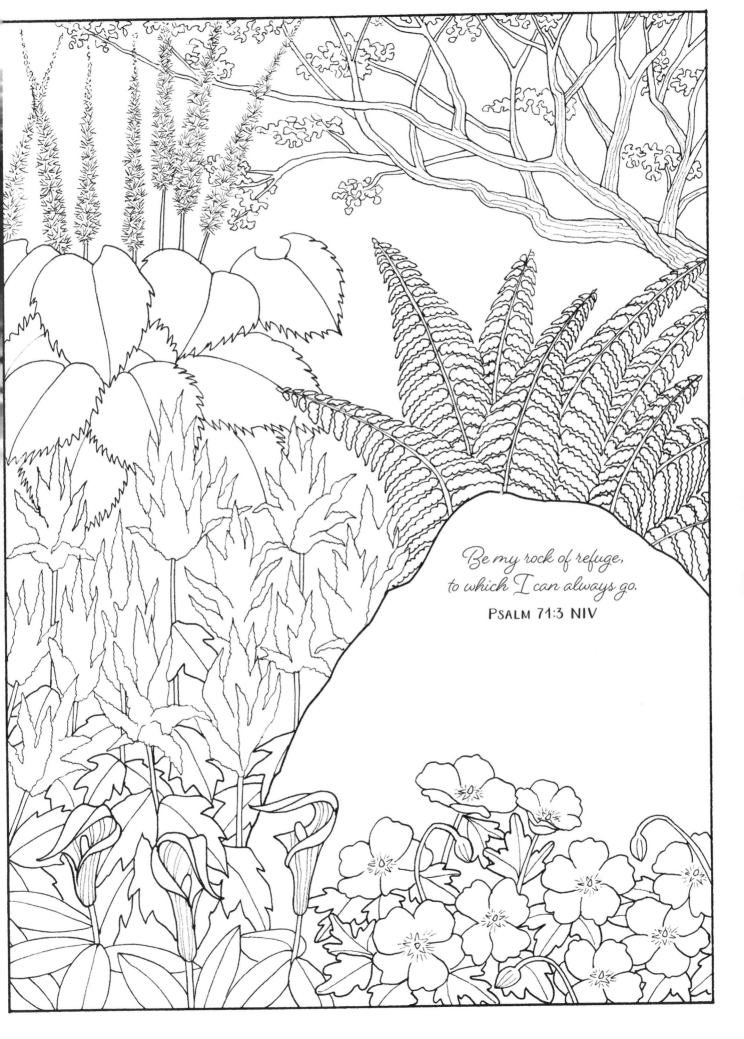

Be my rock of refuge,
to which I can always go.
PSALM 71:3 NIV

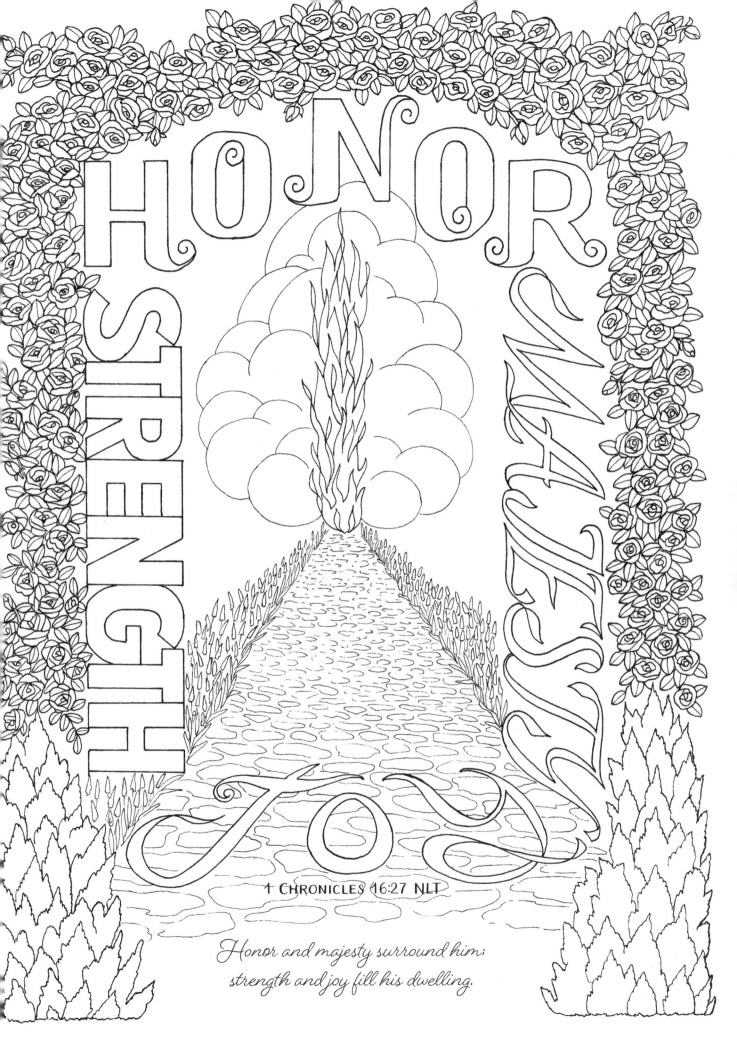

HONOR MAJESTY STRENGTH JOY

1 CHRONICLES 16:27 NLT

Honor and majesty surround him;
strength and joy fill his dwelling.

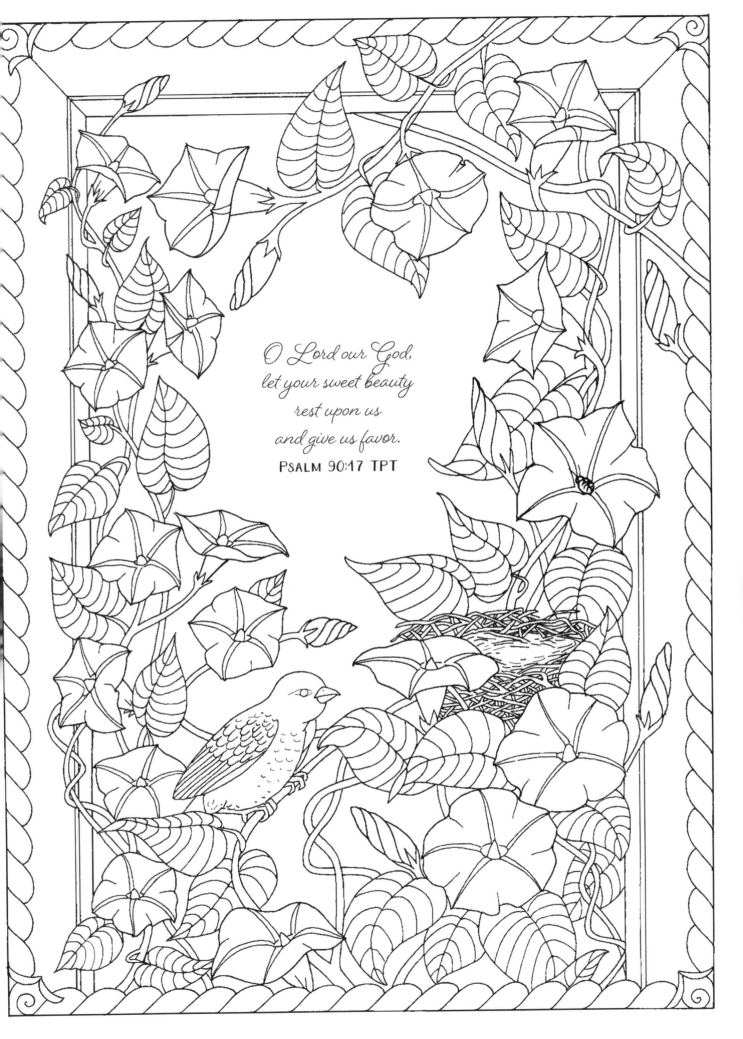

O Lord our God,
let your sweet beauty
rest upon us
and give us favor.

PSALM 90:17 TPT

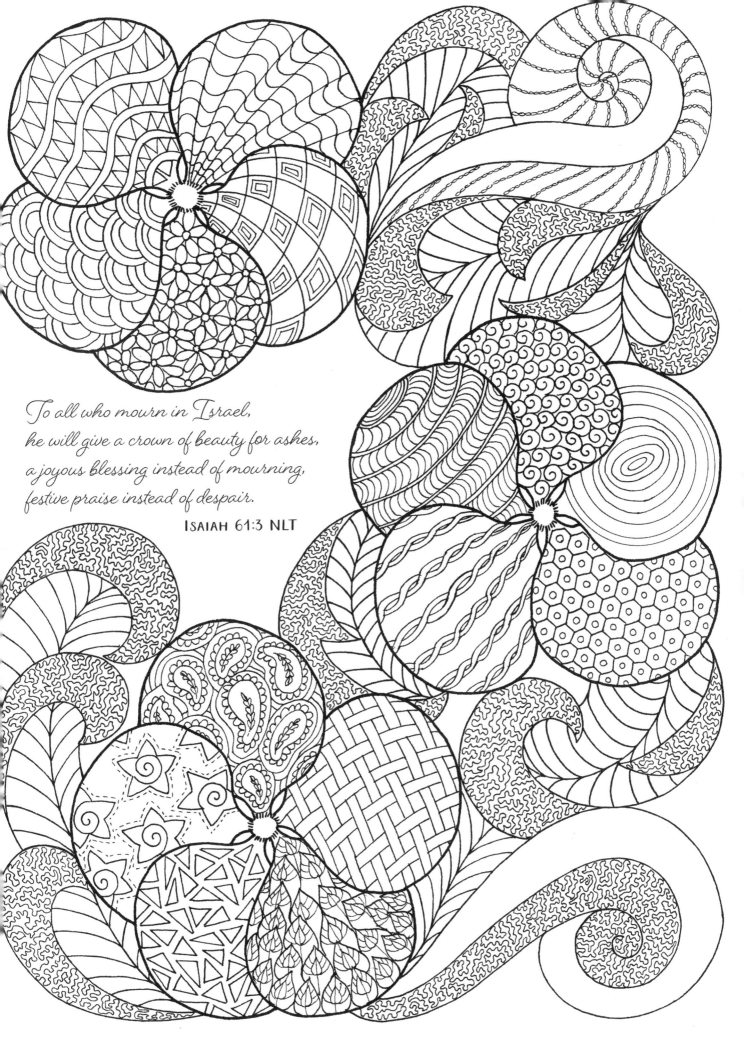

To all who mourn in Israel,
he will give a crown of beauty for ashes,
a joyous blessing instead of mourning,
festive praise instead of despair.

ISAIAH 61:3 NLT

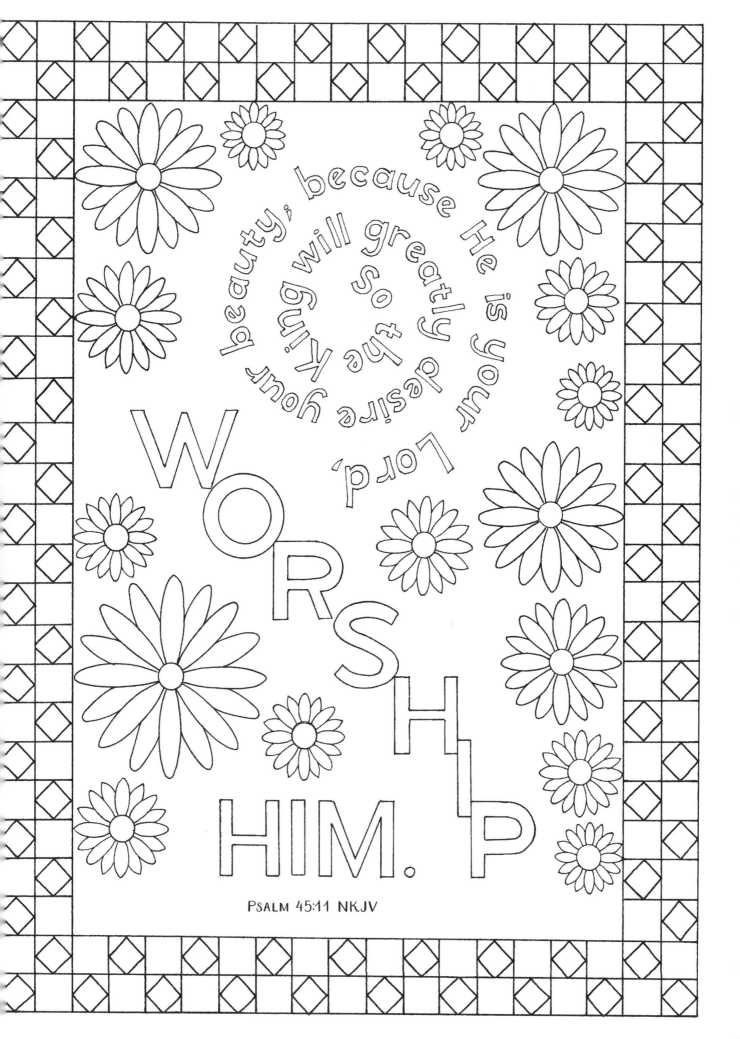

So the king will greatly desire your beauty; because He is your Lord, worship Him.

PSALM 45:11 NKJV

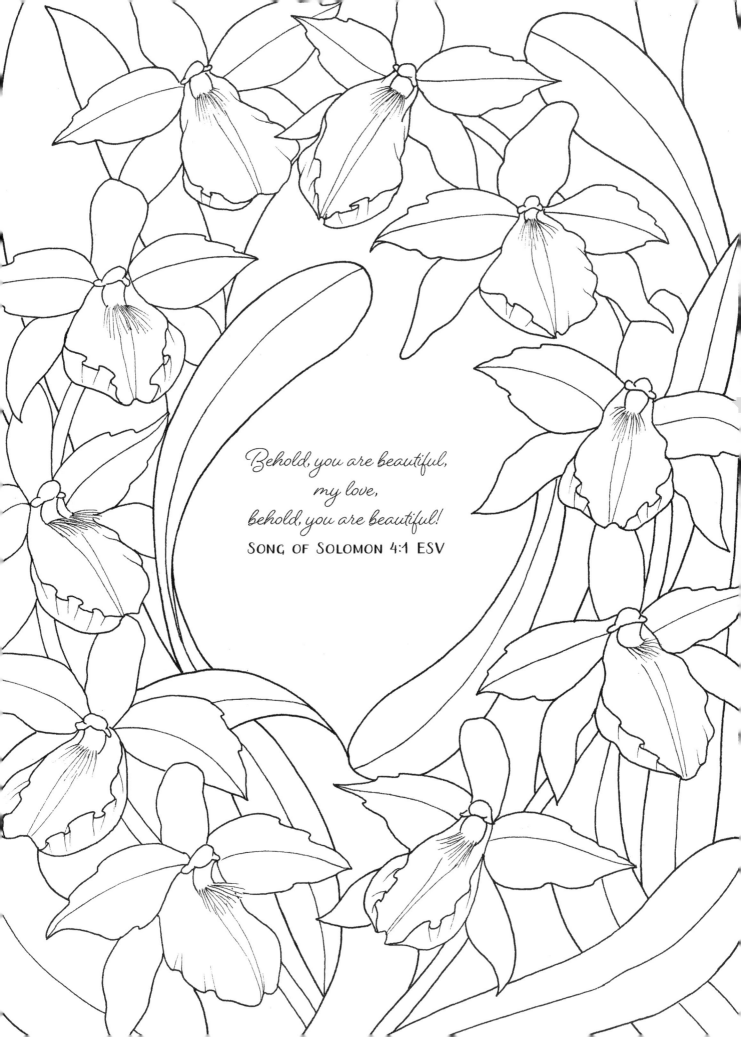

Behold, you are beautiful,
my love,
behold, you are beautiful!
SONG OF SOLOMON 4:1 ESV

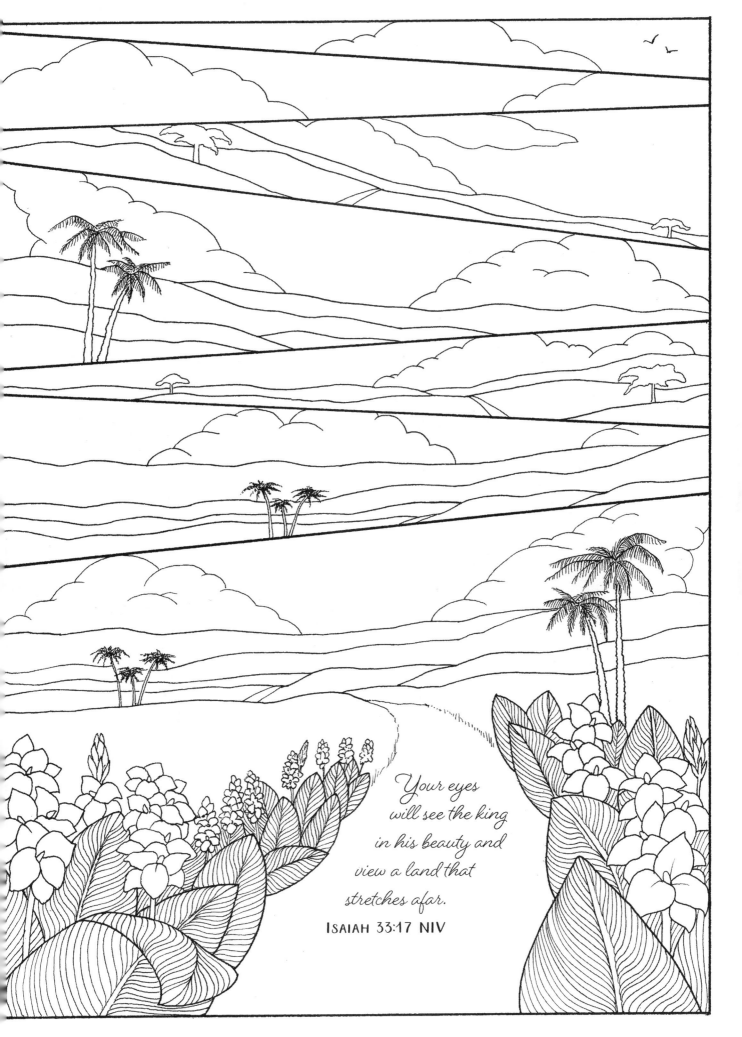

Your eyes
will see the king
in his beauty and
view a land that
stretches afar.

ISAIAH 33:17 NIV

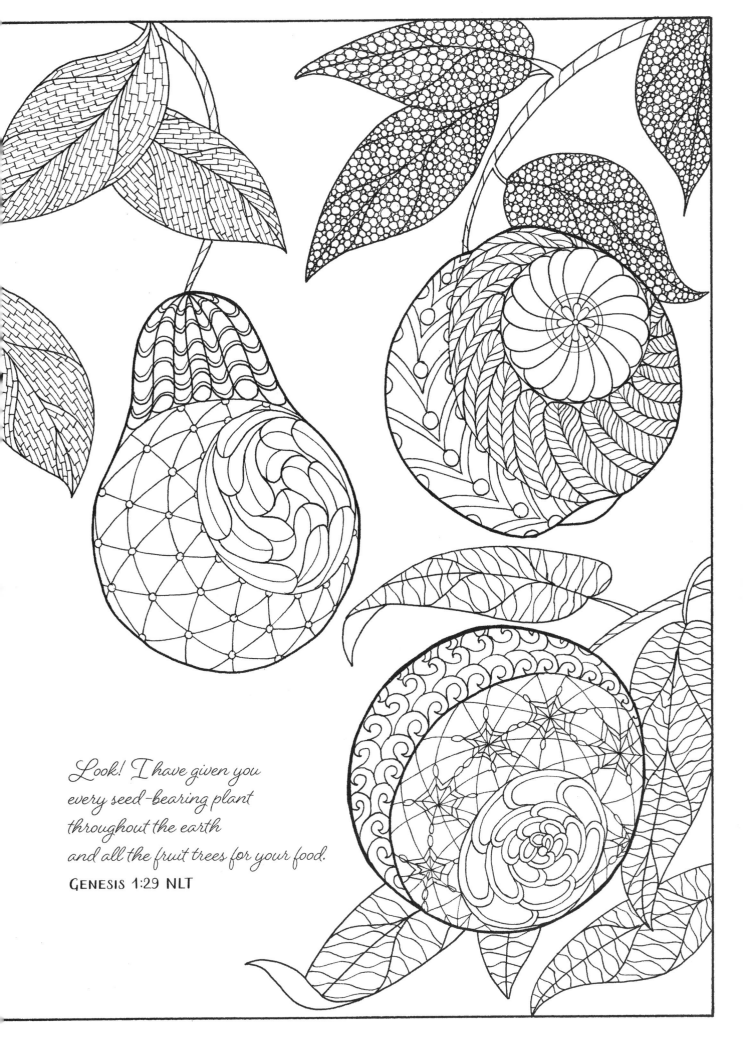

Look! I have given you
every seed-bearing plant
throughout the earth
and all the fruit trees for your food.
GENESIS 1:29 NLT

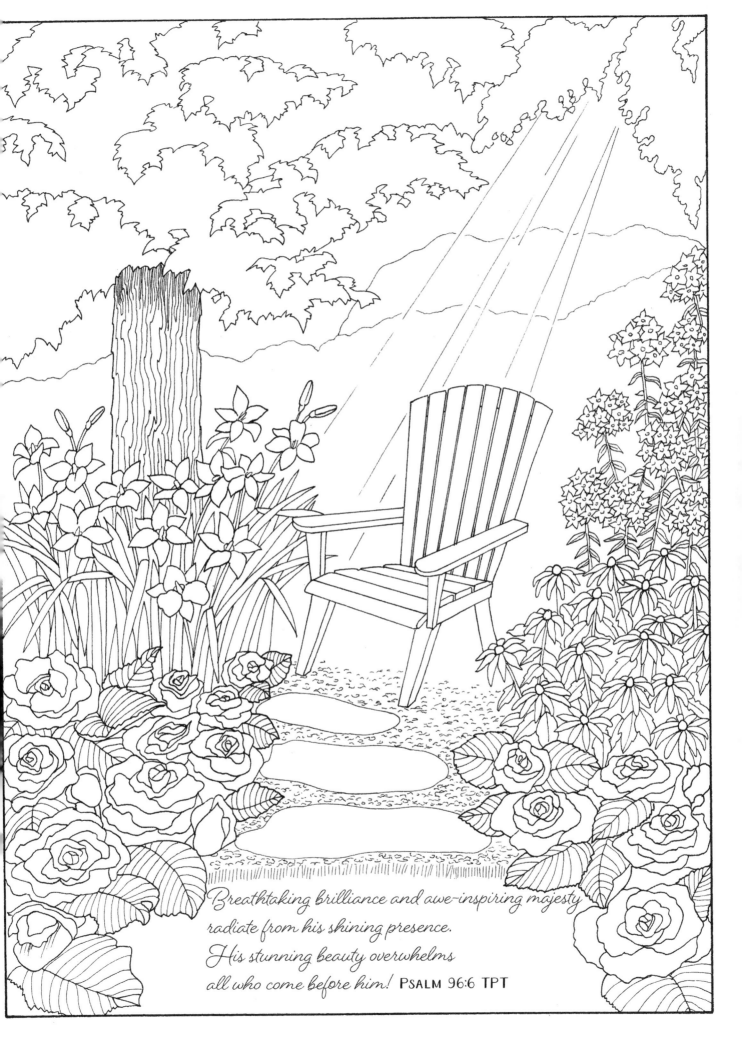

Breathtaking brilliance and awe-inspiring majesty radiate from his shining presence. His stunning beauty overwhelms all who come before him! PSALM 96:6 TPT

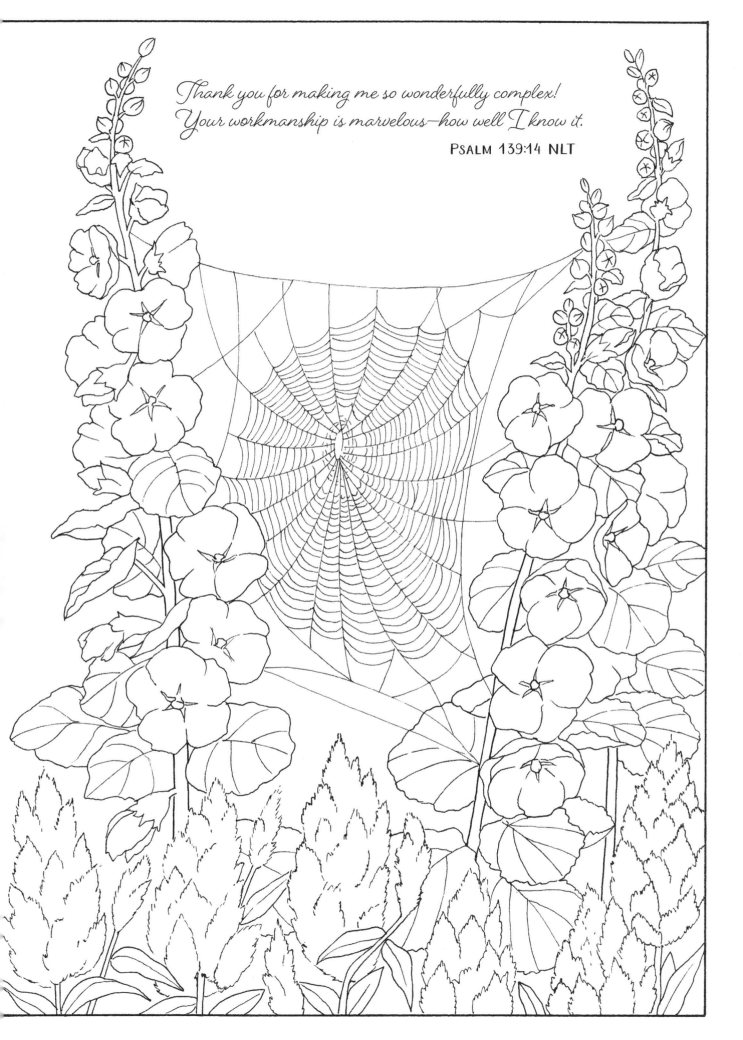

Thank you for making me so wonderfully complex!
Your workmanship is marvelous—how well I know it.

PSALM 139:14 NLT

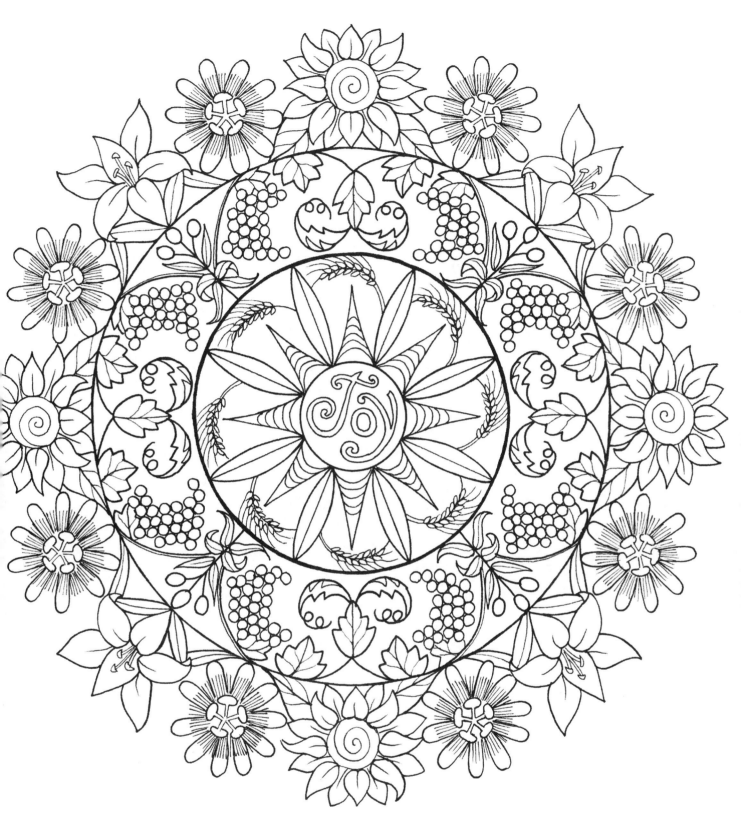

They will come and shout for joy on the heights of Zion;
they will rejoice in the bounty of the Lord—the grain,
the new wine and the olive oil, the young of the flocks and herds.
They will be like a well-watered garden, and they will sorrow no more.

JEREMIAH 31:12 NIV

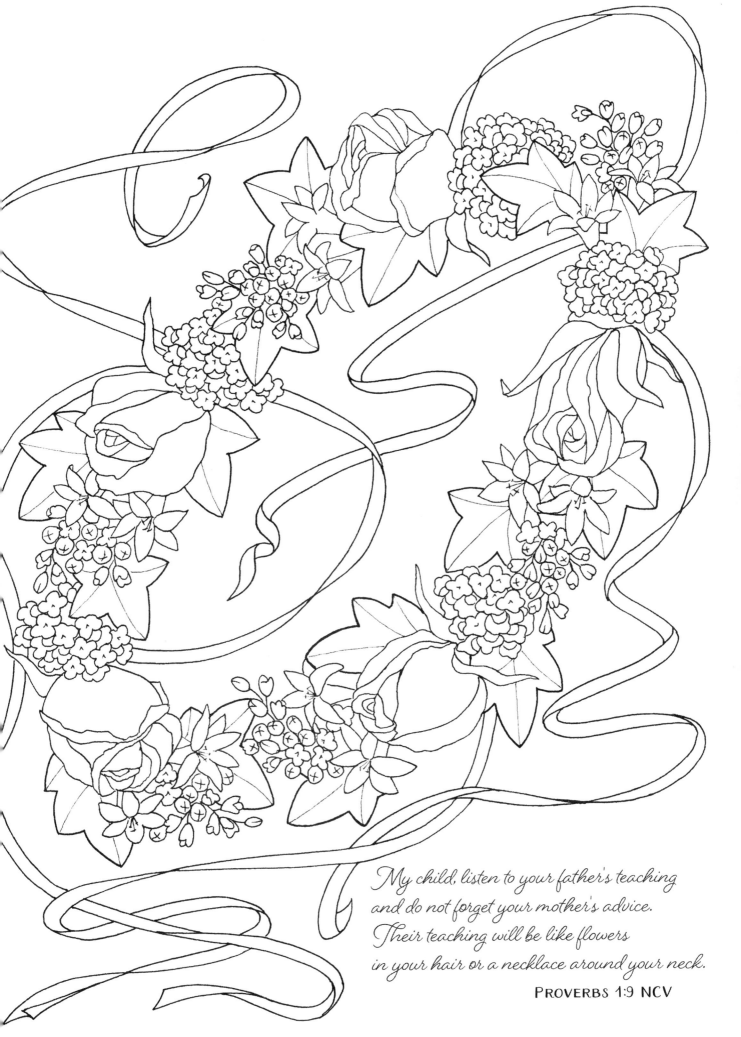

My child, listen to your father's teaching
and do not forget your mother's advice.
Their teaching will be like flowers
in your hair or a necklace around your neck.

PROVERBS 1:9 NCV

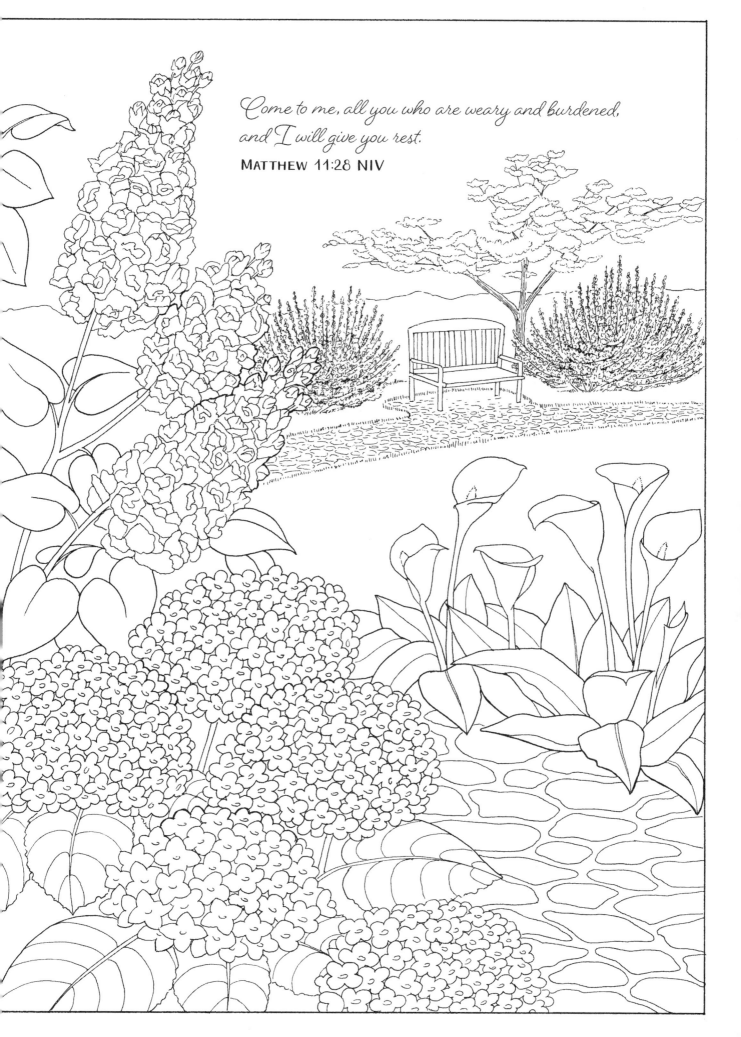

Come to me, all you who are weary and burdened, and I will give you rest.

MATTHEW 11:28 NIV

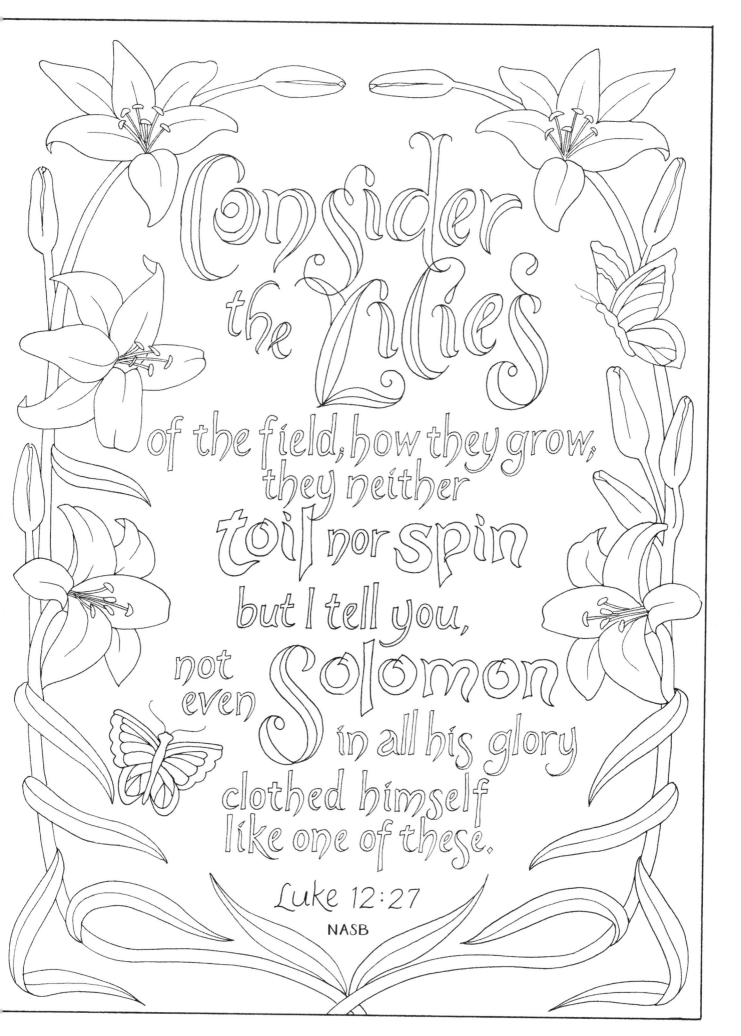

Consider the Lilies of the field, how they grow; they neither toil nor spin but I tell you, not even Solomon in all his glory clothed himself like one of these.

Luke 12:27

NASB

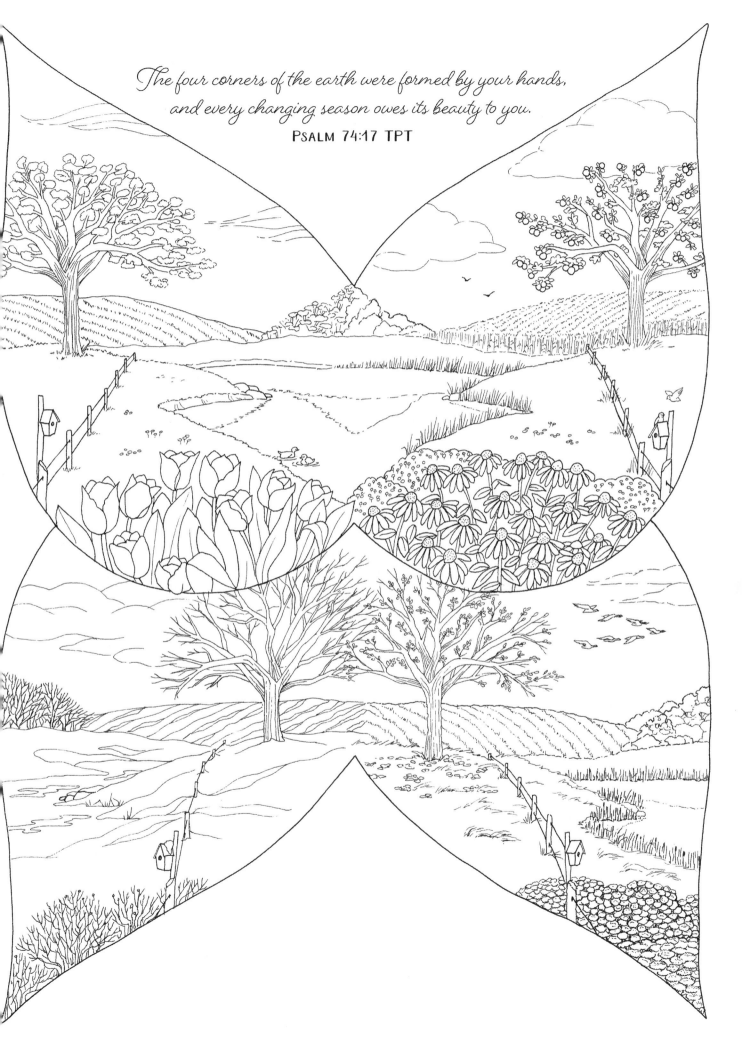

*The four corners of the earth were formed by your hands,
and every changing season owes its beauty to you.*

PSALM 74:17 TPT

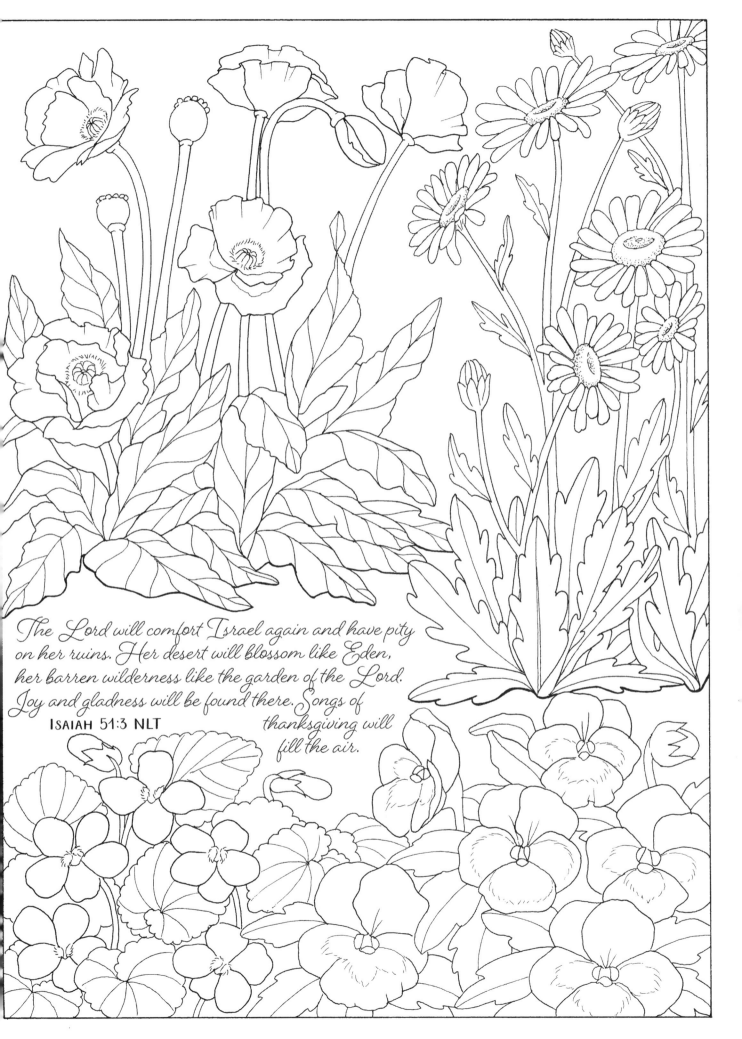

The Lord will comfort Israel again and have pity on her ruins. Her desert will blossom like Eden, her barren wilderness like the garden of the Lord. Joy and gladness will be found there. Songs of thanksgiving will fill the air.

ISAIAH 51:3 NLT

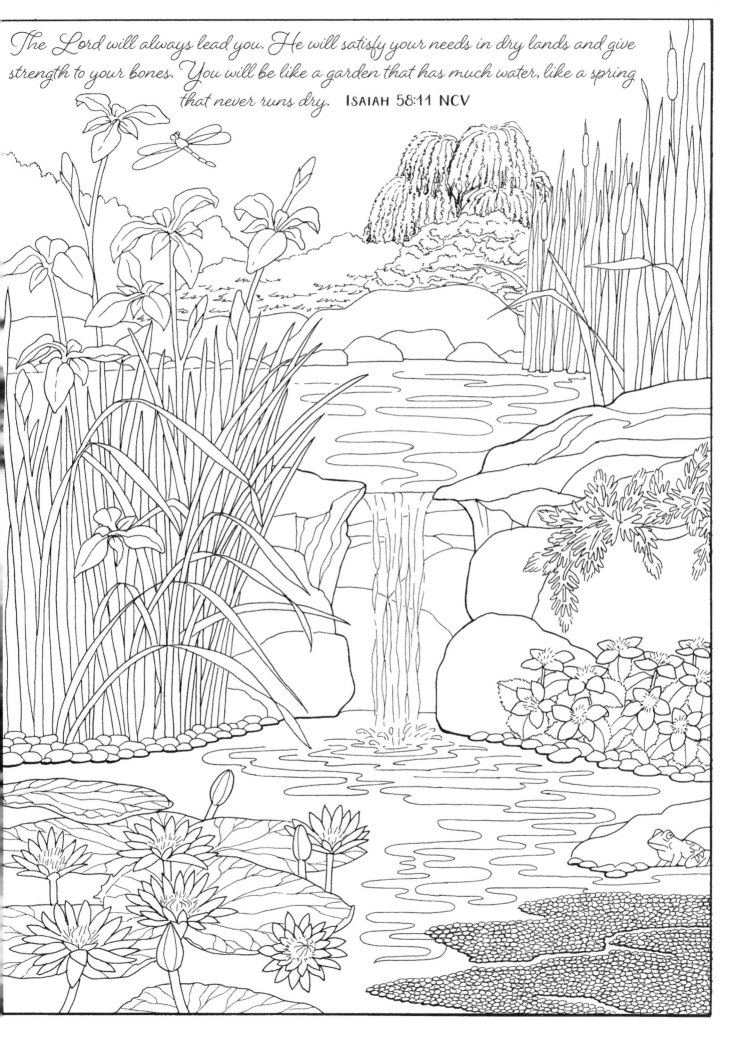

The Lord will always lead you. He will satisfy your needs in dry lands and give strength to your bones. You will be like a garden that has much water, like a spring that never runs dry. ISAIAH 58:11 NCV

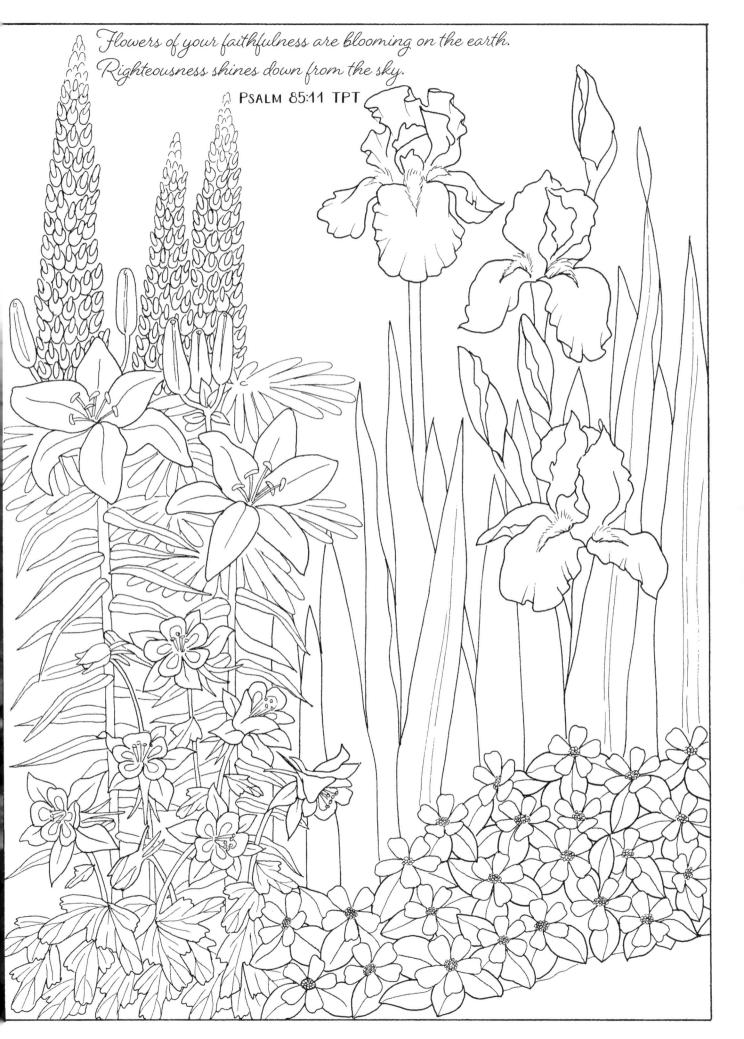

Flowers of your faithfulness are blooming on the earth.
Righteousness shines down from the sky.
PSALM 85:11 TPT

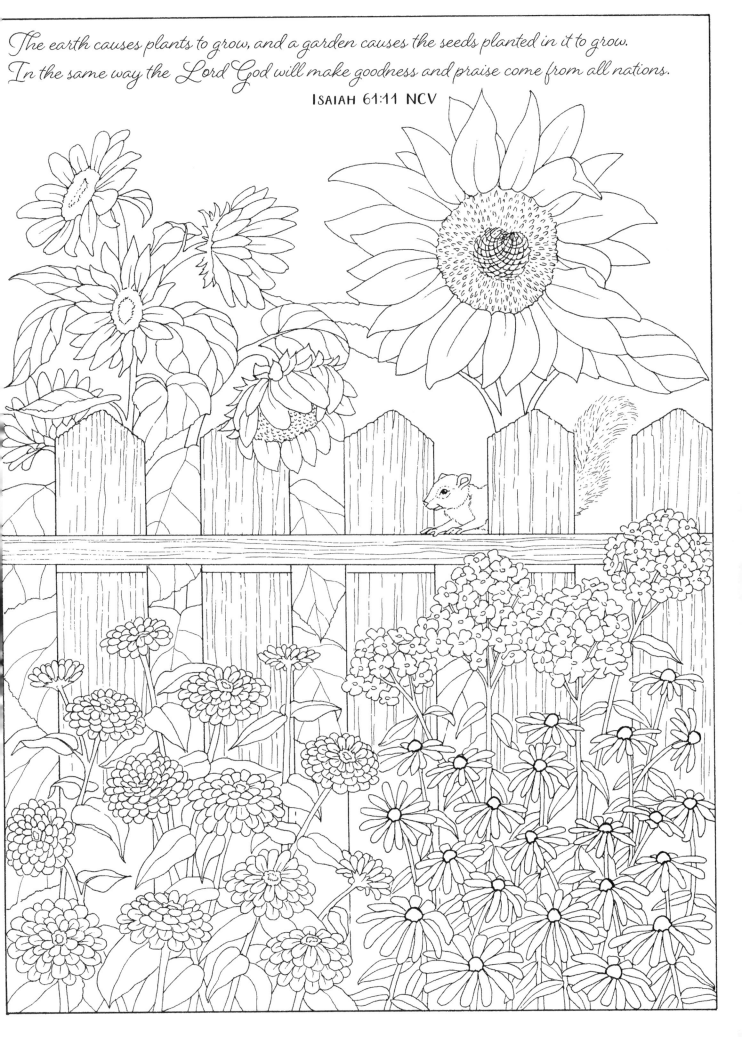

The earth causes plants to grow, and a garden causes the seeds planted in it to grow.
In the same way the Lord God will make goodness and praise come from all nations.

ISAIAH 61:11 NCV

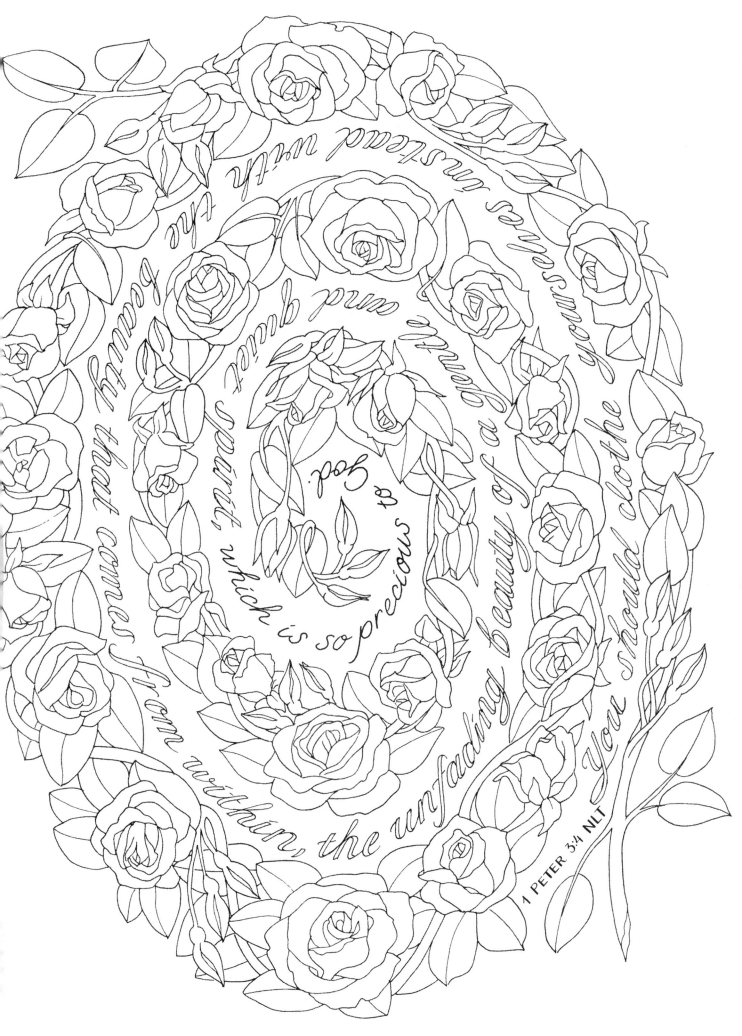

You should clothe yourselves instead with the beauty that comes from within, the unfading beauty of a gentle and quiet spirit, which is so precious to God.

1 PETER 3:4 NLT